Creative PAINT FINISHES FOR FURNITURE

PHILLIP C. MYER

NORTH LIGHT BOOKS
CINCINNATI, OHIO

A NOTE ABOUT SAFETY

Due to the toxicity concerns, most art and craft material manufacturers have begun labeling their products with proper health warnings or nontoxic seals. It is always important to read a manufacturer's label when using a product for the first time. Follow any warnings about not using the product when pregnant or contemplating pregnancy, about keeping the product out of reach of children or about incompatible products. Always work in a well-ventilated room when using products with fumes.

The information in this book is presented in good faith, but no warranty is given, nor results guaranteed, nor is freedom from any patent to be inferred. Since we have no control over physical conditions surrounding the application of products, techniques and information herein, the publisher and author disclaim any liability for results.

CREATIVE PAINT FINISHES FOR FURNITURE
Copyright © 1996 by Phillip C. Myer. Manufactured in China. All rights reserved. No part of this book may be reproduced in any form or by any electronic or mechanical means including information storage and retrieval systems without permission in writing from the publisher, except by a reviewer, who may quote brief passages in a review. Published by North Light Books, an imprint of F&W Publications, Inc., 1507 Dana Avenue, Cincinnati, Ohio 45207. (800) 289-0963. First edition.

This hardcover edition of *Creative Paint Finishes for Furniture* features a "self-jacket" that eliminates the need for a separate dust jacket. It provides sturdy protection for your book while it saves paper, trees and energy.

Other fine North Light Books are available from your local bookstore, art supply store or direct from the publisher.

03 02 01 00 99   7 6 5 4 3

Library of Congress Cataloging-in-Publication Data

Myer, Phillip C.
    Creative paint finishes for furniture / by Phillip C. Myer.
        p.   cm.
    Includes index.
    ISBN 0-89134-636-8 (alk. paper)
    1. Furniture painting. 2. Texture painting. I. Title.
TT199.4.M94   1996
749—dc20   95-20553
                                                          CIP

Edited by Julie Wesling Whaley
Designed by Sandy Conopeotis Kent
Cover photographs by Michael LaRiche

The listing of credits and acknowledgments on page 128 constitute an extension of this copyright page.

DEDICATION

This book is dedicated to an inspiring teacher and friend, Priscilla Hauser. Priscilla's love for decorative art and her willingness to share her painting knowledge continue to inspire me after a business and friendship association of over twenty years.

SPECIAL THANKS

I would like to thank the following individuals for their assistance with the development of this book:

- Andy Jones, for design and creative inspiration
- Michael LaRiche, for photography
- Pat Worrell, for decorative painting support
- Chris Williams, for stenciling work
- Wanda Carter, for base painting
- Carol Myer, for sewing assistance
- John McDonald of Back Street, Inc., for glazes and products
- Dee Silver of Silver Brush Ltd., for brush development
- Margo Christensen of Martin/F. Weber Co., for paints and products
- Rene Erickson of Khoury, Inc., for furniture acquisition
- And to all my students who continue to inspire me through their painting growth and development

ABOUT THE AUTHOR

Phillip C. Myer has been painting for over twenty-four years. He is the author of *Creative Paint Finishes for the Home* as well as eight softcover books on tole and decorative painting techniques. A member of the Society of Decorative Painters for over eighteen years, Phillip teaches seminars across the United States and at his Atlanta based studios. Phillip and his business partner, Andy Jones, create custom-painted furniture and interior decorating through their business—PCM Studios.

TABLE OF CONTENTS

New Decoupage

see page 91

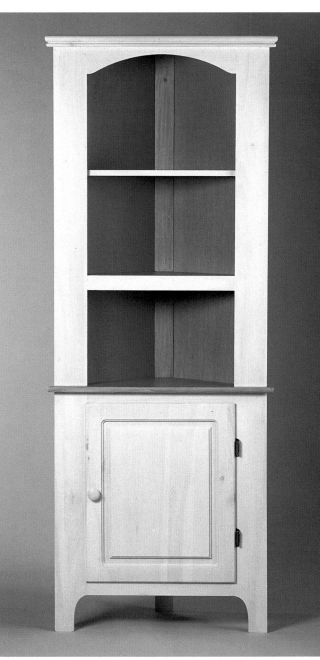

Pickling
see page 19

INTRODUCTION

Painted furniture has grown in popularity to become an important part of the interior decorating of today's homes. There is no easier way to spice up a room than with a decoratively crafted piece of painted furniture. Painted furniture blends well with just about any decorating style you are working with, from country to contemporary. A well-designed furniture surface can tie a room together, creating harmony by repeating a pattern or design, a texture or color, or a style or mood. Mixing your decor with a combination of painted and stained furniture creates a great deal of interest in your home. Decorating a room with *all* painted or *all* stained furniture can look very stiff and stilted.

With the popularity of "nesting" (creating a pleasing, cozy and inviting home environment) in contrast to our fast-paced, high-tech world, we want to establish a retreat to rest and feel comfortable at home. The explosion of "do-it-yourself" trends is the reaction to this need to create this environment within a reasonable budget. Creating your own painted and designed furniture falls into this category.

By completing these decorative treatments you will be creating one-of-a-kind furniture pieces to be passed down your family as a superb heirloom. You will have the option of taking an older piece of furniture and giving it a face-lift by updating it with fresh color and designs. The expense you'll incur in creating the decorative paint treatment is low when compared with the value of the finished piece of furniture.

You may be asking, "Where do I begin?" Well, right in your home, attic or garage there is a piece of furniture you no longer find attractive. Take that piece of furniture and let it become your starting point. If you are unhappy with it now, there is little you can do to make the situation worse, right? Use this as your learning piece. If you fail on this one or don't achieve the finished results the first time, you've lost little. Remember, you are working with paint and brush, and just about everything you do with these techniques can be sanded down and repainted. Learn from your mistakes—this is how creative individuals grow.

After you've experimented with the relics in your home and created a magical transformation, you'll want to begin decorating a new, unfinished furniture piece. These new pieces will provide you with a "ground zero" level to lay a foundation upon and build up with any type of decoration you desire. Once you've completed several pieces of furniture, word will spread among your family and friends, and soon they will place requests for you to revive their "plain" looking furniture. Watch out! Painting furniture can become addictive, but I'm sure you'll learn and grow through the experience and redecorate your own "nest" in the process. Good luck.

Phillip C. Myer

A great starting point in experimenting with painting techniques for furniture is the creation of sample boards. Using hot press (smooth finish) illustration board, you can work with paints and tools to acquire a feel for the methods. You'll be able to determine the right color combination for your home's decor and provide a practice lesson for yourself before tackling the furniture piece at hand. These sample boards will become great reference materials for future projects.

CHAPTER 1
BEFORE YOU BEGIN

Many of the tools used throughout this book can be found around your home. Some techniques will require special tools and brushes. Of these, your brushes will be the most important. Good quality brushes are needed in many cases to create finished pieces. You can use less expensive miscellaneous tools and achieve an interesting look, but without chisel-edged brushes, you'll fight to achieve a good end result.

Tools, brushes and paints will last a long time if cared for properly. Take your time in the finishing and cleanup stages of your project.

PAINTS, PRODUCTS AND VARNISHES

All the furniture projects in this book have been completed with environmentally friendly, water cleanup, acrylic or latex base products. These products are nontoxic, have low to no odor, and clean up easily with soap and water.

Acrylic Paints

To create a variety of color mixtures, a set of artist's grade or student grade acrylic paints in true artist's pigments will be helpful. Permalba Artist's Acrylic Colors or Prima Acrylics in the following colors provide you with a basic palette to make any color combination: Cadmium Yellow Light, Yellow

You can complete all the techniques in this book using water-based products like these.

Ochre, Cadmium Orange, Cadmium Red Light, Cadmium Red Medium, Cerulean Blue Hue, Cobalt Blue, Ultramarine Blue, Dioxazine Purple, Alizarin Crimson, Phthalo Green, Permanent Green Light, Raw Sienna, Burnt Sienna, Burnt Umber, Raw Umber, Titanium White and Mars Black.

Acrylic or Latex Base Paints

You'll need to have a selection of base paints (base coats) to provide a foundation for your decorative finishes. Following instructions for each technique, you'll use either a flat or semigloss acrylic or latex base paint. You can have these colors mixed at a hardware store or home improvement center. Today, most house paint departments have the capability to complete computer color machining. They match a color swatch from your fabrics, wallpaper, carpet or other reference

materials. On small to medium size pieces of furniture, a quart of paint should provide you with two to three coats of base paint for the surface. On larger pieces (armoires), you should purchase a gallon of paint to base coat.

Acrylic Glazing Medium

With the growth in popularity of creative paint and faux finishes, just about every paint manufacturer has produced a water base glazing medium to create color glazes. Some of these products are sold in a clear form so you can tint the glaze to create your color mixture. Others are pretinted with color. You want a product that has an open time (working time) to manipulate the wet glaze and paint in the desired technique. You should have a minimum working time of fifteen minutes and maximum working time of forty minutes.

You can make acrylic glazing medium by mixing water base polyurethane varnish plus acrylic retarder plus water. Place equal amounts of these three products in a jar and stir thoroughly. You'll use this as the base clear acrylic glazing medium to which artist's acrylic colors or house acrylic or latex paints are added to create a transparent color glaze.

Ready-Made Glazes and Base Coats

You can find a selection of ready-made color acrylic glazes with co-ordinating base coat colors. Anita's Beginners' Glaze System provides the novice with a preselected and coordinating opaque base color with a transparent color glaze. These are available in a selection of twelve colors: Sand/Dark Brown; Goldenrod/Eggshell; Ecru/Indian Brown; Mushroom/White; Fog/Black; Red Oxide/Gold; Midnight Blue/Edgewater Blue; Pale Pink/Poppy Red; Burgundy/Rose; Seafoam Green/Forest Green; Sky Blue/Dark Williamsburg; Black/Silver.

Copper Topper and Patina Green

These two products have been designed to create the look of oxidized copper. They imitate what happens in nature when a greenish patina develops on copper through corrosion. Although the cleanup with these two products is soap and water, they are not totally acrylic base products. Copper Topper has copper metal particles suspended in emulsions and binders. Patina Green is made up of oxidizing chemicals. Carefully follow directions for use.

Decoupage Glue

To complete the gluing steps found in several techniques, a decoupage glue is required. Decoupage glue is a white craft glue with a thin consistency. Glue that is thick will not work for these methods. You can take a fluid, white craft glue and thin down with additional water to a flowing consistency.

Foil Adhesive

Adhesive designed for the application of foil gilding comes in a water cleanup form. This glue brushes on the surface in liquid form, sets and becomes sticky. This provides a base for the foil gilding to adhere to the surface.

Water Base Varnishes

Water base polyurethane varnishes are used throughout the techniques found in this book. They provide durability, broad open time, water and alcohol resistance. Finishing furniture pieces with different techniques such satin, semigloss or gloss provides variety to your work.

Spray Finishes

Spray finishes are a final clear coat applied to protect the painted surface. They are manufactured in several forms. Today, there are water-based environmentally friendly sprays. Spray finishes are available in acrylic-based products. Choose satin, semigloss or gloss sheen levels to coat your furniture surface.

BRUSHES

As you build your technique repertoire, you can build your brush collection. There are several brushes that are considered "workhorses" because they are used in just about every technique. These brushes will get used over and over, but if taken care of, they will last a long time. All brushes listed here as examples are produced by Silver Brush Limited. Other manufacturers' brushes can give similar results.

Base Coat Bristle Brush

This is a 3-inch brush made of natural hairs. The brush hairs are cut at a taper angle, which forms a sharp, chisel edge. This edge allows you to stroke a straight line, control base paint application, work the brush into tight spots, and stroke on a smooth, even base coat.

Brushes needed (clockwise from bottom left): several sizes of stencil brushes; golden natural-synthetic blend in flat shaders, rounds and liners; silver mop brush; blending softener brushes; flogger brushes; varnish brush; glaze brush; base coat bristle brush; and polyfoam brushes.

Glaze Brush

The glaze brush is 2 inches wide and made from soft, natural hairs. This brush is made with a tapered cut like the base coat brush. The natural hairs soak in sufficient amount of glaze to allow you to stroke out a fair amount of color glaze to the surface. Synthetic hair brushes do not provide this control because the artificial hair cannot drink in moisture.

Varnish Brush

A 1-inch brush made of natural hair allows you great control when loading on a water base varnish. The hairs drink in the varnish then release it when you apply pressure with the brush. This size brush enables you to get varnish into tight, recessed areas.

Flogger Brush

This style brush is made of a combination of natural and synthetic hairs measuring 5 inches in length beyond the metal ferrule. This brush produces unique marks in the wet paint glaze. The long hairs can create strie, flogging and dragging techniques.

Blending Softener Brush

This brush is made from soft, natural goat hair. Available in 1-, 2- and 3-inch sizes, it provides fine blending techniques. The soft hairs of this style brush allow you to move paint and blend with great ease.

Silver Mop Brush

The mop brush is a size no. 14 made of soft, natural hairs and allows the same qualities of the blending softener brush but enables you to get into specific areas to control the blending techniques.

Golden Natural Flats

Flat brushes in sizes no. 8, 14 and 16 provide a range needed to complete detail work. These brushes are made from a combination of natural and synthetic hairs. They have sharp, chisel edges to access specific areas. They paint a clean, sharp edge or line on a surface.

Golden Natural Round

A no. 4 round brush is needed for detail and touch-up work when a fine-pointed brush is required. Made of natural and synthetic hairs, it will hold a good deal of paint.

Golden Natural Script Liner

A script liner in a no. 1 size will provide crisp line work. A script liner is different from a standard liner brush due to the length of its hairs. Script liner hairs are about ½ to ¾ inch longer. This extra hair length holds more paint and creates a longer detail line.

Silver Stencil Brushes

Stencil brushes made from coarse hog hair provide the stiffness necessary to create dimension in your stencil work. Sizes from no. 4, 8, 10 and 14 are needed.

Foam Brushes

Polyfoam brushes in 1-, 2- and 3-inch sizes are ideal for trim and some base coat painting. They can also be used to apply glue. Do not use them for varnish application; a natural hair varnish brush provides better results.

TOOLS AND MATERIALS

The following tools are used in the techniques throughout this book. Refer to the supply listing found with each technique in chapters three to seven to determine what you need.

Tracing Paper

Transparent tracing paper comes in pad form (12" × 16") or roll form (24 inches long). This will be used for tracing and drawing pattern designs, as well as a foundation material in the leather look technique.

Palette Knife and Paint Stirs

A palette knife with a long, wide blade is required to thoroughly mix the paint and glaze. The blade should be flexible. Use wood paint stirs to mix quarts and gallons.

Wax-Coated Palette and Styrofoam Plates

The palette (12" × 16" with wax coating) and the Styrofoam plates (with no divided sections) will provide you with surfaces to mix small amounts of acrylic or latex paint and acrylic color glaze.

Metal Rulers

Rulers in 12- and 36-inch lengths with a corked backing will be used for measuring and ruling pen work.

Ruling Pen

A ruling pen can be filled with thin consistency paints to draw a fine trim or detail line. It has a slot area for filling with paint and a turn screw to adjust line width.

Craft Knife

A craft knife with a sharp blade will come in handy for cutting and scoring surfaces. It is ideal for cutting stencils.

Stencil Burning Tool

This is a special tool for cutting through acetate or Mylar by use of

a heated point. It is perfect for the creation of intricate and multiple stencil overlays.

Brayer

A rubber-based brayer will roll over a surface and apply pressure to smooth out an area. It is handy for laying decoupage prints and sections of torn paper.

Decoupage Scissors

Small scissors with curved and straight blades are required to cut out prints. They should have sharp blades.

Burnishing Tool

A burnishing tool with a hard plastic, chisel edge is handy to rub down tape when masking out an area to paint. A tip of a large metal spoon will provide similar results.

Foil

Foil for gilding techniques is available in gold, silver and copper, in roll form.

Chicken or Duck Feathers

Fine-pointed chicken feathers are required to place the vein structure in some marbleizing techniques.

Permanent Markers

Fine point markers with permanent ink in colors of black and brown can

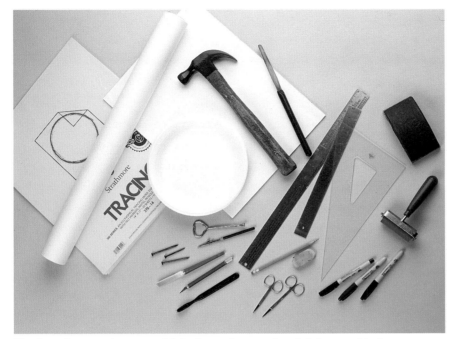

Tools and materials required (clockwise from mid-right): brayer, black permanent markers, decoupage scissors, pencil and eraser, toothbrush, craft knife, burnishing tool, nails and screws, ruling pen, paint key, tracing paper (pad and roll), Styrofoam plates, wax-coated palette, hammer, palette knife, rulers, triangle and sanding block.

Miscellaneous Items

The following items are standard household and painting workshop tools. Many relate to a specific technique taught in this book. Check the project supply list for necessary tools.

- Paint key to open cans
- Pencils
- Erasers
- Toothbrush
- Nails
- Screws
- Triangle
- Hammer
- Plastic gloves
- Cotton rags
- Cheesecloth
- Bar soap
- Paper sacks
- Dense foam
- Hot glue gun and glue sticks
- Clear acrylic spray
- Drop cloths
- Sanding block
- Mop bucket
- Murphy's Oil Soap
- Denatured alcohol
- Wood putty
- Spackling compound
- Putty knife
- 3M's Safest Stripper
- Paste wax
- Acrylic gel medium
- Acrylic retarder
- Containers—small and large "butter" tubs

provide fine detail lines in several techniques, including marquetry.

Tapes

Several types of tapes are required when painting. They should all be repositionable, which will allow you to pull up the tape and realign without harming the coating below.

3M's white safe release tape and blue long mask tape prevent paint seepage as you brush along the masked area. Easy Mask's brown painter's tape provides an adhesive on half of one side of the tape.

It is much wider, for broader coverage and protection of the masked area.

Sandpaper

A variety of sandpaper in coarse, medium, fine and ultrafine (400- and 600-grit) grades are required to smooth out surfaces.

Steel Wool

Fine (#0000) steel wool can be used in creating a "glasslike" finish on your varnish surface.

- Wallpaper paste
- Acetone
- Tack rag
- Gray graphite paper
- White transfer paper

BASIC HOW-TO'S

There are a few basic principles that apply to most projects you'll be working on when creating your furniture decoration. Read the following information to prepare yourself for the painting adventures that lay ahead.

Base Coating

An important step in finishing a piece of furniture will be applying a base paint to the surface. It is critical this foundation color go on in a smooth fashion. To achieve a good, smooth and even base coat coverage, you should follow a few easy tips: Load the base coat bristle brush with plenty of paint, saturating the bristles with color, then lightly stroke both sides of the brush's bristles against the rim of the paint container to remove excess paint. You need to coat from the chisel edge of the brush up the bristles about 1 to 2 inches. Once the brush's bristles are loaded with paint, begin stroking color on the surface. Tackle one section of the furniture at a time. Apply paint into recessed trim areas first, then pro-

ceed to the larger span areas. Paint in long, fluid strokes—short, choppy strokes make for a messy looking base coat and can be magnified when decorative treatments are placed over them. Apply one coat and let dry thoroughly. Follow the drying schedule found on the paint label. If you do not allow proper curing time, the next coat can sag and cause curtaining.

Cleaning Brushes

Once you have invested in good quality brushes, it is important to take care of them. When you are not using a brush for a period of time and it has paint and glaze in it, you should stop and clean it. Water base products dry rapidly even when mixed with retarders. So when you are done painting a section, place brush in a container of water and when done for the day, take your brushes to the sink and wash them thoroughly with soap and water. Murphy's Oil Soap cleans the acrylics and glazes out of your brushes. Rinse the brush, and wash a second time to verify that all traces of color have been removed from the brush's hairs. The hairs of the brush go much farther past the metal ferrule, and you want to remove any paint that may be residing there. Shake off excess moisture and allow to dry.

If you've allowed acrylic to dry in the brush's hairs, a small amount of acetone will work some or all of the dried acrylic out of the hairs. Note, the acetone may be harmful to certain types of brush hairs.

Developing Paint Glaze Consistencies

When you create your own paint glazes for the techniques taught in this book, you'll be creating transparent mixtures at different thicknesses. Here are some guidelines to mix your glaze to the proper consistency:

Thick, creamy consistency. Prepare a mixture of 20 percent acrylic glazing medium and 80 percent paint. The paint should be thick enough to form peeks when you pat the palette knife over it.

Thin, creamy consistency. Prepare a mixture of 40 percent acrylic glazing medium and 60 percent paint. The paint should be mixed to the consistency of whipped cream.

Thin, soupy consistency. Prepare a mixture of 70 percent acrylic glazing medium and 30 percent paint. Mix glaze and paint to a creamy, tomato soup consistency.

Inklike consistency. Prepare a mixture of 80 percent acrylic glazing medium and 20 percent paint. As the name implies, the consistency should be watery and inklike.

Glaze Mixing

You'll create some type of transparent color glaze for most of the techniques found in this book. Depending on the materials and paints you'll use to create the glaze mixture, there are several approaches to achieving the proper mixture. Here are the best procedures:

Mixing From Artist's Tube Acrylics. Often, you'll mix a small quantity of paint and glaze to create a specific color. Working with artist's acrylic colors allows you to work with strong, intense colors that can be mixed to any color combination, color value, color intensity and paint consistency. Begin by squeezing a half dollar size of paint from the tube onto a Styrofoam plate. Slowly begin to add the acrylic glazing medium. Using your palette knife, "mash" down the thick pigment to mix the paint in with the medium until you begin to develop a fluid consistency. Then begin to add additional quantities of the acrylic glazing medium until you achieve the desired paint consistency. See Developing Paint Glaze Consistencies.

Mixing From House Paints. House paints (interior flat, satin, semigloss or gloss acrylic or latex paints) are already in a fluid state, so less mixing will be required. Using an old container (butter tubs work well), pour in about a quarter cup of paint. Now, slowly add the acrylic glazing medium, and stir the mixture with a paint stir. Check for the level of paint consistency by stroking out paint on a scrap surface. Add more acrylic glazing medium to achieve proper paint consistency and transparency level. If you need more body in the mixture, add acrylic gel medium. See Developing Paint Glaze Consistencies.

Flyspecking

One of the simplest paint techniques is the addition of color through the method of flyspecking. This technique achieved its name from the tale of early master craftsmen finding that flies would walk across their paint palettes and then distribute small tracts of paint over their painted furniture.

To achieve this look (without the assistance of flies), thin paint with water or acrylic glazing medium to the consistency of ink. Using an old, stiff bristle toothbrush, load the tip of the bristles with the inklike paint. Holding the toothbrush's handle in the center of your palm, direct the loaded bristles downward and run your thumb across the bristles. Paint flecks will fall from your toothbrush. The closer you get to the surface, the larger the paint flecks will become; the farther away, the smaller the flecks.

Watch out not to overload the toothbrush with too much paint—large paint "blobs" will drop to the surface. If this occurs, simply wipe away excess with a moist paper towel. See Foil Gilding (chapter five).

Trim Painting

You must not overlook an important step in the finishing of your painted treatment on the furniture surface—trim painting. Through the addition of color trims and color bands on the furniture's edges, legs, routed areas, molding or carved details, you'll "flush out" the overall finished effect of the furniture project. These areas offer opportunities to repeat colors used in the main design work and thereby create a cohesive look. You can freehand paint these areas using a no. 12 golden natural flat brush, or you can tape and mask out surrounding areas before painting trim areas.

CHAPTER 2
SURFACE PREPARATION

The first step in creating a decorative treatment on a piece of new or old furniture is the proper preparation. You must take care to seal the underlying surface, and prepare the substratum (the underlying layer), which all topcoats will need to adhere to. If you rush this process and do not prepare and seal the surface for future coatings, your topcoats can easily be damaged, knotholes can bleed through the painted surface, and paint reactions such as peeling, cracking or crazing can occur.

The type of surface you're about to decorate will determine the steps required to prepare the substratum for your decorative topcoats. The two major categories for furniture preparation are new, unfinished wood furniture and finished wood furniture. The latter can be finished furniture that is relatively new or a piece of furniture with greater age (something from Grandmother's attic). Furniture pieces can also be made from other nonwood surfaces or particle wood (wood chips formed together with glue). They need to be prepared in a similar fashion.

Other surfaces that are popular for painted decoration are plaster and pottery. Columns, corbels, planters, obelisks, niches and shelves are now being made in a variety of shapes, styles and sizes in both plaster and pottery materials. These surfaces can become great accent or accessory pieces to be used in conjunction with your larger furniture pieces. These types of surfaces require a few preparation steps to result in a fantastic finished result. A few basic preparation materials are required for getting the furniture surface ready for the painted decoration. You'll need cleaning materials: sponges, rags, cleaning agent (Murphy's Oil Soap or denatured alcohol), gloves, sponges, bucket of water; patching compounds: wood filler, spackling compound, putty knife or palette knife; smoothing agents: sandpaper (fine, medium and coarse), sanding blocks, brown paper grocery sack, steel wool, tack rag; primers and sealers: water base or oil base primer (such as Kilz), tannin block sealer.

PREPARING NEW, UNFINISHED FURNITURE

Unfinished furniture is available in a variety of shapes and sizes at an unfinished furniture store or home improvement center. This type of furniture is most commonly made from pine, but you can find ready-made unfinished furniture in a hardwood such as oak. Another source for unfinished furniture can be a local woodworker who may make

---

Keys to Success

* Start sanding with a coarse to medium grade of sandpaper, and then work down to fine grades. The coarser the grade of paper, the faster you will level rough areas, while the finer sandpaper will finish smoothing the surface.
* Be sure to fill in imperfections, such as dents and nail holes, with wood filler (for areas to be stained) or spackling compound (for areas to be painted).
* Strip a surface only when the piece has financial or sentimental value. Consider having the piece commercially stripped.
* Read the instructions for the technique you wish to use. Certain techniques require special preparation and base coating procedures.
* Always take the time to correct problems on the substratum (the foundation), such as peeling paint, loose veneer, cracked or broken wood. Applying new paint or stain over these problems will not correct or hide them; it will magnify them.

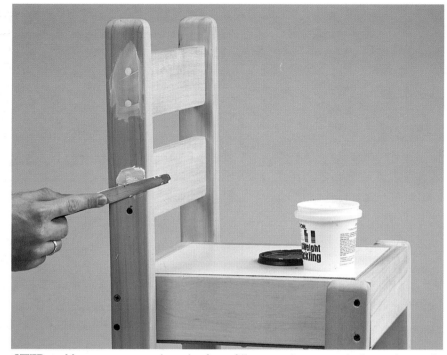

STEP 1. Use a putty or palette knife to fill any nail or screw holes with wood putty or spackling compound. Also fill dents or damaged areas at this time. Let compound set up and dry following product label's instructions.

unusual, one-of-a-kind pieces, selling them at art and craft shows or through specialty gift shops. Locating a local source will allow you to have a specific piece of furniture made in the style, size and type of wood of your choice.

Once you've found the piece of unfinished furniture, the next step will be deciding on what type of technique you would like to complete over the raw wood. Since the wood is untreated, you have the greatest selection of techniques, from staining techniques found in chapter three through all other techniques taught in this book. Here are the steps to follow for unfinished wood for staining or painting.

Staining Preparation for New Wood

Review the new piece of furniture by checking the surface for any major imperfections, such as dents or valleys near knotholes. These areas may need to be filled in with a wood putty. Use a putty product that will accept stains. Fill in recessed areas with putty using a putty or palette knife. Let dry. After the putty is dry, sand surface with a fine piece of sandpaper.

Depending on the craftsmanship of the unfinished furniture piece, you'll have a great deal of sanding on a roughly finished wood piece or a minimum amount on a nicely crafted piece. Run your hand around the surface to feel for rough

spots—routed areas, end grain areas or roughly planed areas. For flat rough surfaces that require sanding, load a strip of coarse sandpaper on a sanding block. Stroke the sanding block with the direction of the grain of the wood. Complete sanding on all rough areas. Now, change sandpaper on the block to a medium grade, repeat sanding of all former rough areas, and lightly sand all remaining areas. To access recessed routed or curved areas, wrap sandpaper around your fingers and stroke with sandpaper. Finish by sanding all surfaces with a fine grade of sandpaper. Once all sanding is completed on the furniture piece and all surfaces are smooth to the touch, you'll need to remove sanding dust. Pick up a tack rag and wipe down the surface before proceeding to the decorative staining techniques taught in chapter three.

Painting Preparation for New Wood

Raw wood that you intend to paint will require a few extra steps. It is critical that you seal and prime the wood surface so in the future no visible grain or knotholes bleed through the surface. You'll need to look over the surface to locate any areas that need patching and repair work (dents, recessed knotholes, recessed nail holes). Since you will be covering the surface with paint, you can use the new lightweight spackling compounds that are on the market. They dry rapidly and sand

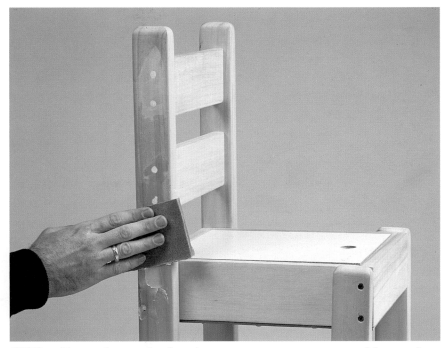

STEP 2. Using a fine grade of sandpaper, remove excess compound from surface, leveling out to a smooth surface. Sand all other areas of the furniture at this time. Remove sanding dust with a tack rag. If you plan on a stained finish, the surface is ready to stain.

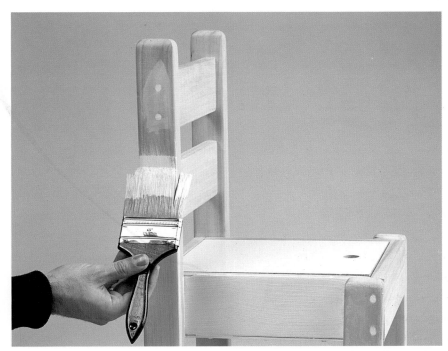

STEP 3. If you plan on a painted finish, you'll need to prime the surface with a stain blocking primer, such as Kilz. Brush on a smooth coat with base coat brush. Let dry and sand. Recoat with primer. The surface is now ready to be base coated with your color of choice.

well. Fill in holes with spackling compound using a putty or palette knife. Let dry. Using a fine grade of sandpaper, sand over the patched areas to level them with the surrounding surfaces.

Now, sand the entire surface to level out rough spots. Depending on the coarseness of the wood, work from coarse or medium grade down to fine grade sandpaper. Remember to always sand in the direction of the wood grain. After the surface is completely sanded and smooth, you'll need to remove sanding dust with a tack rag.

The wood surface to be painted will need to be primed and sealed. You can use a tannin block sealer for wood pieces that have a great deal of large visible knotholes. Brush on tannin block sealer on just the knothole areas. This type of sealer is so strong it can almost seal a surface too much (if completed on the entire piece). Let tannin block sealer dry following label's instructions. After the knotholes are sealed, prime the wood to prepare the surface to accept your topcoats. Primers such as Kilz, a stain blocking sealer and primer, will need to be brushed on the surface. Using the base coat bristle brush, stroke the primer on all areas of the furniture surface. Let dry. The moisture from the primer will cause the wood grain to rise and feel rough. To knock this down, lightly stroke over the surface with a sanding block and fine grade of sandpaper. Remove

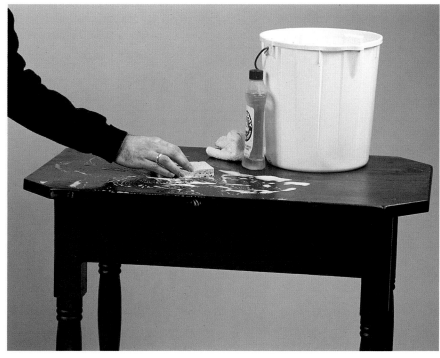

STEP 1. The surface needs to be washed thoroughly to remove all dirt, grease, oils and debris. Fill a bucket with water and cleaning agent, and wash surface with a kitchen sponge. On extremely glossy surfaces, you'll need to wash with a solution of water and denatured alcohol.

sanding dust with tack rag. Recoat with primer. Let dry. Your new, primed wood surface is now ready for paint. Select the base coat color, and proceed with your decorative paint technique.

PREPARING FINISHED FURNITURE

Whether the finished furniture piece is relatively new or is old, you'll need to prepare the finished surface for future coating. The biggest difference between new and old is usually the amount of dirt and oils that need to be cleaned off the surface. You may also want to strip down the furniture surface to raw wood to complete any of the stain-

ing techniques taught in chapter three. Stripping the finish is not necessary unless you want to stain the wood or the existing finish is peeling and cracking off the surface. Stripping the surface is very involved, so you'll need to be committed to the work ahead or have it commercially stripped.

If the end result is any type of painted finish and the existing finish is intact, you do not need to strip the surface. You'll need to remove dirt and oils by cleaning, sand the surface to create a tooth to the surface for your new topcoats to grab hold of and prime the surface before going on to base coating and decorative treatments.

Stripping Furniture

Stripping furniture is a messy job and one that takes time, so be sure the furniture piece is worth this extra step. There are new environmentally friendly stripping products, such as 3M's Safest Stripper, that are ideal for use by the do-it-yourselfer. These new products are nontoxic and odor free and don't harm your skin. Always read the instructions found on the manufacturer's label.

Begin by testing stripper on a small section of the furniture piece (drawer front). This will give you a quick indication of how many layers of varnish, stain or paint exist on the surface. If the surface is currently painted, you may be surprised; the surface may be made of all types of scrap wood or from a beautiful veneer pattern.

Once you've decided to strip the furniture piece, gather the following supplies: stripping product, old brush, a stack of newspaper, gloves, putty knife, toothbrush, steel wool, electric sander, drop cloth and garbage bags. Work outside or in a well-ventilated area and not near important surfaces. Lay drop cloth on floor, and layer newspapers over drop cloth. Place furniture on the center of the papers. Brush the stripper on one section at a time (preferably a horizontal area). Following the reaction time of product, let stripper activate on surface. After the stripper has activated the top layer(s), you can scrape off the coat-

STEP 2. Sand the surface to create a tooth that the topcoating will adhere to. Use a medium grade of sandpaper and a sanding block. Sand with the direction of the grain. Remove sanding dust with a tack rag.

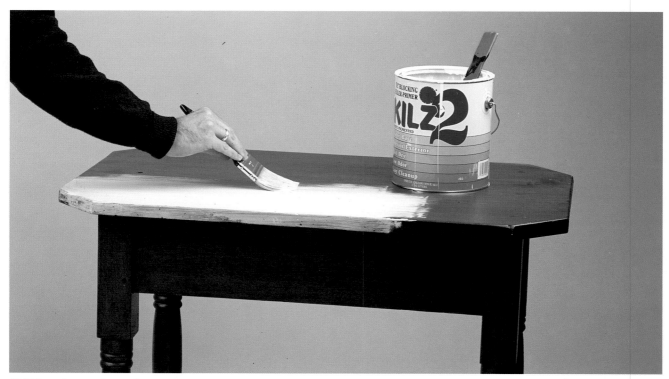

STEP 3. Prime the surface with a stain blocking primer and sealer. This will prevent the former finish from telegraphing through to the new finish. Apply a primer with a base coat bristle brush in fluid, long brushstrokes across the furniture surface.

STEP 1. Wipe the dust from the surface with a moist sponge. Clean sponge often in fresh water. Be sure to clean out the deep recesses of the piece.

grooves in the existing paint or varnish will establish areas for the top-coating to hold and "bite" into. Do not complete sanding with a fine grade of sandpaper. Remove sanding dust with tack rag.

You'll need to prime the surface to keep underlying colors, stains or varnish coatings from coming through your new coats. Use a stain blocking primer, such as Kilz. Brush on a coat with the base coat bristle brush. Let dry. Sand lightly with a fine grade of sandpaper, and remove dust with tack rag. Recoat with primer. You are now ready to determine paint finish technique and proper base coat color.

ing with the putty knife. Place discarded coating on newspapers.

Recoat with stripper until you activate and scrape off all layers of the coatings. Use a toothbrush to access carved details. Once a majority of the coatings have been removed, rub surface with fine steel wool. Complete these steps for all sides of the furniture surface. Let surface moisture dry. Sand the stripper residue. An electric sander will come in handy for larger areas. You can now prepare the surface for stained or painted effects following the instruction for new wood preparation.

Painting Preparation for Finished Wood

You'll need to begin by cleaning the surface with a cleaning agent such as Murphy's Oil Soap. Fill a bucket of water and pour in several capfuls of the cleaning agent. Load a kitchen sponge with the soapy water, and scrub down the surface to remove dirt and oils. If the finished surface is fairly old and extremely slick, make a mixture of water and denatured alcohol (60:40 ratio) in a bucket. The denatured alcohol will cut the glossiness of the surface, providing a better tooth to hold topcoats.

Once you've removed all dirt and oils and cut any glossiness on the surface, sand the surface to rough up the paint or varnish that currently exists on the surface. Begin with a medium grade of sandpaper. Stroke the sandpaper on the surface in a slightly rough fashion. Small

PREPARING JUNK FURNITURE

Furniture that would fit into a "junk" category would be pieces that have seen their better days—pieces with some construction problems, massive paint peeling and chipping problems and overall dated looks. The benefit to junk furniture is that it is usually free—left abandoned, left out for trash pickup or given away. There are several specific techniques taught in this book that can disguise junk furniture and really create a magical transformation. The leather look, distressed finish and torn paper techniques can hide a multitude of problems. The two basic preparation steps prior to applying these techniques on a "junk" piece are cleaning and repairing. First, wash the piece with water and a cleaning agent, such as Murphy's Oil Soap. Clean the debris, grease and dirt off the surface. Repair any areas that need fixing. Glue or nail the broken sections. (Large clamps may come in handy in gluing sections of the furniture back together.)

PREPARING PLASTER AND POTTERY SURFACES

The plaster and pottery surfaces, such as columns, corbels, planters, obelisks and decorative shelves, will require a few simple steps to get them ready to receive a paint finish treatment. Due to the fact that many of these pieces are made from molds, you'll have surfaces with intricately recessed areas (especially on columns) that will require care in cleaning, priming and painting.

Begin by wiping down the plaster or pottery surface with a moist kitchen sponge. Rinse your sponge in a bucket of fresh water from time to time. Do not saturate the surface with water—only remove dust. Let moisture on surface dry for several hours. Next, prime the surface with a good quality primer, such as Kilz. Brush on a smooth, even coating using the base coat bristle brush. Let dry and recoat. Lightly seal the surface with several light coats of clear acrylic spray. You are now ready to begin base coating the surface with the color of your choice.

STEP 2. Seal the surface with a coat of primer. Brush on a coat with base coat bristle brush. Let dry. Recoat the surface with primer and let dry.

STEP 3. Choose the technique of the paint finish to be applied to the surface. Apply appropriate base coat color in a smooth, even fashion. Let dry and reapply base color until an opaque coverage is achieved.

CHAPTER 3
STAINING TECHNIQUES

Pickling
Gel Staining/Marquetry
Clear Coats
Multitone Staining

The richness achieved through staining a piece of furniture made of a beautiful wood grain cannot be matched through paint. To cover up a beautifully crafted wood surface with paint is a great waste. The subtleties of each type of wood and its grain are fascinating to study. You can experiment with the different hues and what they do to each type of wood to achieve an endless selection of finished effects. In this chapter, four distinct staining techniques have been tackled. Each provides a whole set of unique characteristics.

You can choose from simple, clean effects, such as pickling or clear coating, to more pattern or design active approaches of marquetry or multitone staining. All of these techniques can take on entirely different looks by simply changing the colors used to stain the wood surface. Experiment by creating effects ranging in value from dark to light.

These four techniques—pickling, gel staining/marquetry, clear coating and multitone staining—allow the beauty of the wood grain to shine through the tinted color on the surface.

PICKLING

To apply a pickle finish to a piece of wood furniture means to coat the surface with a transparent color wash that is a soft, non-earth tone. The most popular pickling technique uses white, but pickling can be completed in muted tones of virtually any color. Currently, green, blue, pink and soft yellow are popular pickling colors. This technique yields a softness not achieved through traditionally earth tone staining methods.

Pickling must be completed on unfinished or stripped, raw wood. You cannot pickle over an existing finish. Casual rooms, such as kitchens, sun rooms and family rooms, are best suited for pickled furniture, floors, built-in cabinetry and accessories.

PREPARATION

When working on new, unfinished wood, you will need to sand the surface smooth. When working with a wood surface that already has an existing finish, you will need to strip off all finishes until you get down to the raw wood. Be sure all stripping residue is removed, and sand surface smooth.

Optional color ways to make pickling stain: right, Light Old Rose Pink; center, Bright Celadon Green; left, Robin's Egg Blue.

MATERIALS NEEDED:
- Paints—desired colors in acrylic or latex semigloss or artist's acrylic colors (*Sample project features white and Edgewater Blue latex paints*)
- Brushes—glaze brush, varnish brush
- Acrylic glazing medium
- Water base varnish
- Paint stir
- Container—large tub
- Sandpaper
- Tack rag
- Cotton rags

Keys to Success

❈ Test the transparency level of your pickling stain on the underneath side of the furniture surface. Each type of wood will accept the pickling color differently. Hardwoods do not "drink in" much pickling color, while softwoods accept more color.

❈ When pickling over a stripped surface, be sure to remove all areas of the former finish. The new pickling finish is transparent and will not cover up what existing finish is on the surface.

❈ If the first layer of pickling dries too light in value, you can brush on a second coat for a stronger level of color.

PICKLING

STEP 1. Mix equal parts of acrylic glazing medium and water base varnish in tub. Stir well. Slowly add desired color to this clear mixture. You can develop the pickling finish to a variety of transparency levels. Test transparency level by brushing on scrap surface or underneath side of furniture. Add more color if mixture is too transparent; add more clear glaze and varnish if mixture is too opaque. Load glaze brush and begin stroking on wood.

STEP 2. Finish brushing on surface following the natural direction of the grain of the wood. Coat entire area of one section (for example, drawer front, top of table). Pick up a cotton rag and wipe off excess pickling that does not soak into surface. Continue this procedure until all areas are coated. Let dry overnight.

STEP 3. The pickling finish will cause the grain of the wood surface to rise and become coarse. Next, pick up fine sandpaper and lightly sand surface. If the surface is not too coarse, a piece of brown grocery sack can be used to sand and buff the surface. Always sand in the same direction of the grain of the wood. Remove sanding dust with tack rag.

STEP 4. To protect the pickled finish further, especially on surfaces that will receive great wear (furniture and floors), brush on several coats of water base varnish with varnish brush. Wet sanding can be completed after three coats of finish.

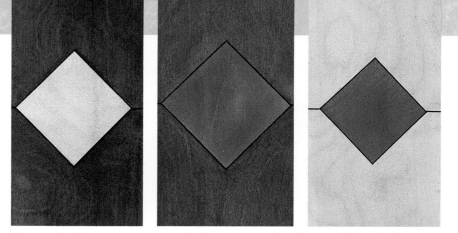

GEL STAINING/ MARQUETRY

Marquetry is an inlay of wood or other material that creates a design or pattern on furniture and small accessories, such as boxes. You can mix different wood color tones on the surface to create elegant designs. The patterns you create can be graphic shapes or specific subjects.

A finished marquetry design tends to provide a "dressy" look, so rooms designed with an elegant or formal feel are appropriate. Furniture and accessories for living and dining rooms and master bedrooms are perfect for the marquetry technique.

Optional color ways to create inlaid sections: right, white and Payne's Gray; center, Burnt Sienna and Gold; left, black and white.

MATERIALS NEEDED:
- Paints—desired colors in acrylic or latex semigloss or artist's acrylic colors (*Sample project features Burnt Umber, Burnt Sienna Raw Umber, Mars Black*)
- Brushes—glaze brush, varnish brush
- Acrylic glazing medium
- Acrylic gel medium
- Water base varnish
- Artist's white tape—repositionable or blue long mask tape
- Permanent markers—fine point brown and black or a variety of earth tones
- Palette
- Palette knife
- Tracing paper
- Pencils
- Ruler
- Triangle
- Gray transfer paper
- Burnishing tool or spoon

PREPARATION

You will need a new, unfinished wood surface or a stripped wood surface that has been sanded smooth. Remove sanding dust with tack rag. Create marquetry design on tracing paper with pencil, triangle and ruler. Establish a color layout by coloring in the design with markers.

Keys to Success
❋ Do not apply much pressure on the pencil as you draw out the marquetry design. Heavy pencil lines and indented pressure on the wood will show up.
❋ Secure tape in place by burnishing the surface. This will prevent the gel stain from seeping under and causing a "bleed-out."
❋ Keep marquetry design simple on your first project. This will allow you to become familiar with technique before tackling larger or more intricate designs.
❋ If color mixture is too thin, excessive bleeding under tape will occur between inlaid sections.

GEL STAINING/MARQUETRY

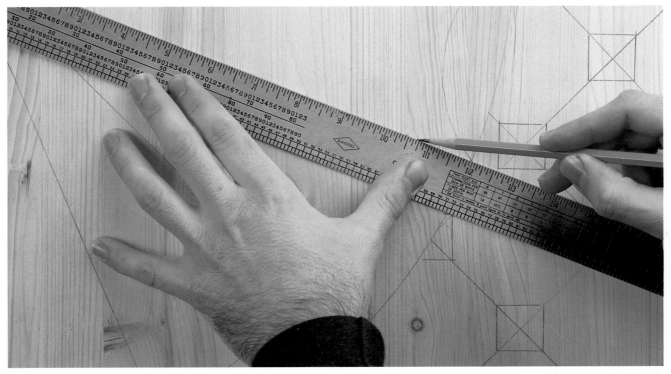

STEP 1. Lay out marquetry pattern on tracing paper. Place on surface and tape into position. Slip transfer paper underneath tracing paper, and lightly go over design lines with a "dead" pen. Remove papers. Go over any light lines with pencil and ruler. Tape off independent sections with repositionable tape. Rub down tape edge with burnishing tool or tip of spoon.

STEP 2. Mix acrylic colors with equal parts of acrylic gel medium and acrylic glazing medium using a palette knife. Depending on the volume of color needed, you can mix color on the palette or in a container. The color consistency should be gel-like and transparent (thick, creamy consistency). Following the color layout, load a glaze brush with color gel or glaze and brush in desired areas. Be sure not to brush forcefully into the tape's edge—this would force color gel or glaze to seep into adjoining area. Let dry.

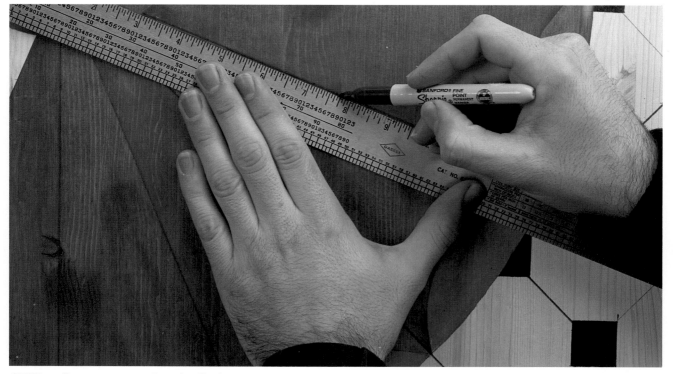

STEP 3. Remove tape and mask off adjoining sections. Place color on these sections following the same procedure. Let dry. To define sections, go over the outside shapes with a brown or black fine point permanent marker. Use a raised ruler to prevent marker from seeping under ruler and causing a blur or color drag.

STEP 4. Coat entire wood surface with water base varnish using the varnish brush. The wood areas that were left untreated will now have a natural wood finish look. The varnish will also bring the grained pattern through the colored areas of the marquetry design. Apply three coats, then wet sand, and then apply a final coat of varnish.

CLEAR COATS

To clear coat a surface means to apply a natural-looking finish to an unfinished wood surface. This technique is desirable when you wish to achieve a clean, colorless look on a piece of furniture. The pattern of the wood grain and any wood markings will be highlighted in this process. Wood knots, worm holes, nick and dents in the wood will not be disguised; they will be accented when you apply a clear coat to the surface.

Furniture, rooms and homes that have casual, simple lines to their architecture are best suited for this technique. Clear-coated accessories and furniture are ideal when designed for rustic rooms, such as dens, porches and country kitchens, and getaway homes, such as lake and mountain cabins.

PREPARATION

To create the clear coat technique, you'll need new, unfinished furniture or old furniture that has been stripped of its existing finish. Sand furniture surface thoroughly to remove any roughness. Begin with a medium grade of sandpaper, and then work with a fine grade of sandpaper. Use a sanding block on flat surfaces. Wrap sandpaper around your finger for sanding trim areas. Remove sanding dust with tack rag.

Keys to Success

❊ If you desire a clean, precise look to the wood surface, take the necessary time to sand away any imperfections in the surface. The clear coat will not hide dents or nicks in the wood.

❊ Be sure to remove all residue on a stripped piece. The clear coat will appear uneven in coloration if you do not remove all of the existing finish properly.

❊ Take your time in the sanding process. It is the key to a flawless clear coat finish. You want to achieve a clear coat look that people will marvel and want to touch and feel.

❊ Take caution when wet sanding; you can sand right down through the varnish very quickly. The wet sanding will leave a hazy, scratched quality to the varnish surface. Don't be alarmed; this will go away when you apply another coat of varnish to the surface.

❊ A minimum of four coats of varnish should be applied to the surface. Additional coats can be added for extra depth in the look and feel of the furniture. Optionally, you could apply three coats, wet sand, apply three more coats, wet sand, and then apply the final coat for a total of seven coats of varnish.

MATERIALS NEEDED:
- Brushes—varnish brush
- Water base polyurethane varnish
- Paint stir
- Wet/dry sandpaper—medium (220-grit) and fine (400- and 600-grit)
- Tack rag
- Soap—bar
- Container of water
- Towel

STEP 1. Be sure to remove all sanding dust after the sanding preparation step. Any residue will adhere to surface and cause excessive roughness. Thoroughly stir water base polyurethane varnish, but do not cause air bubbles to form in can. Dip varnish brush in polyurethane, and begin on one section of the piece of furniture. Coat across the surface allowing the varnish to flow on and overlapping the previous stroke. After section is coated, move to the next section until all areas are coated. Let dry for four hours.

STEP 2. The first application of varnish on the raw wood surface will cause the grain of the wood to rise and create a rough feel to the surface. To remove roughness, lightly sand the surface with fine, 400-grit, sandpaper. Attach sandpaper to sanding block and sand in the direction of the grain of the wood. Remove sanding residue with a tack rag.

STEP 3. Next, apply a second coat of water base polyurethane varnish to the surface; follow the same section by section procedure. This coat of varnish will tend to sit on top of the surface more than the first coat (it may appear more "milky" when wet). Watch out for any varnish runs. Allow varnish to dry four hours or more, and apply a third coat. Let dry for at least four hours.

STEP 4. To achieve a smooth, glass-like finish, wet sand the surface. Use fine, 600-grit, wet/dry sandpaper, a bar of soap, and a container of water. Dip a small piece of sandpaper into water and run across the bar of soap. In a circular motion, lightly sand the surface, and continue to wet the sandpaper and pick up more soap. After entire surface has been sanded, remove soap and sanding residue with a damp towel. Allow to dry. Apply final coat of water base polyurethane varnish to surface.

MULTITONE STAINING

To create this technique, you will actually place several stain colorations on the surface. This procedure can dress up a plain piece of furniture and can highlight the carved, grooved or trim sections of a more elaborately crafted piece of furniture. You can create multi-toned staining techniques in values of the same color or intermix several colors on the surface.

Multitone staining can be created in a serious look for formal rooms (dining and living rooms) or can become playful for casual settings (family rooms) and whimsical settings (children's rooms).

Optional color ways to create multi-tone staining: right, Napthol Crimson with black shading; center, Burnt sienna with Raw Umber shading; left, Yellow Ochre with Burnt Sienna shading.

PREPARATION

When working on new, unfinished wood, you will need to sand the surface smooth. When working with a wood surface that has an existing finish, you will need to strip off all finishes until you get down to the raw wood. Be sure all stripping residue is removed, and sand surface smooth. Remove all sanding dust with tack rag.

MATERIALS NEEDED:
- Paints—desired colors in acrylic or latex semigloss or artist's acrylic colors (*Sample project features Forest Green—Phthalo Green plus Ultramarine Blue plus Raw Umber*)
- Brushes—glaze brush, varnish brush, mop brush
- Acrylic glazing medium
- Water base polyurethane varnish
- Paint stir
- Container—large tub
- Sandpaper—medium (200-grit) and fine (400- and 600-grits)
- Tack rag
- Cotton rags
- Soap—bar
- Container of water
- Towel

Keys to Success
- Be sure to test the value of the stain mixture on an underneath side of the furniture surface. Each type of wood will accept the stain color differently. Hardwoods accept very little color, while softwoods accept a great deal.
- The staining and varnishing steps will cause the grain of the wood to rise. You will need to thoroughly sand between steps.
- To achieve strong contrast between different stain colors on the surface, allow each coating to dry before applying another color. If you wish to achieve a mingling of stain colors, apply colors together on the surface.

MULTITONE STAINING

STEP 1. Mix acrylic glazing medium and water (80:20 ratio) in tub. Stir well. Slowly add desired color to this clear mixture. You can develop the stain to any level of transparency you desire. Test transparency level by brushing on underneath side of furniture. Add more color if mixture is too transparent; add more clear glaze and water if stain is too opaque. Make all color stains following this procedure. Load a glaze brush with stain, and brush on in the direction of the wood grain.

STEP 2. Use cotton rag to remove excess stain from surface by rubbing into wood grain. If you wish to achieve a two-tone layered effect, stain entire surface with one color and allow to dry before applying the second color. If you wish to create a variegated stained effect, rub different stain colors side by side on the surface. Allow first application of stains to dry.

STEP 3. To strengthen stained colors on the surface and develop a two-tone layered effect, create a thicker consistency stain by eliminating the addition of water to the mix. Now, side load the new stain mixture on the glaze brush and stroke into areas of the surface where you desire stronger color. You can highlight furniture edges, corners, trim, molding and carved detail with the thicker stain color.

STEP 4. Soften the darker stain into the wood surface with rag and mop brush. Let dry. Seal and finish the staining by applying a series of coats of water base polyurethane varnish. After the first three coats, wet sand using fine sandpaper, water and soap, and then apply a final coat of varnish.

CHAPTER 4
FAUX FINISHES

Leather Look
Antique Look
Marbleizing
Patina Verdigris

A faux finish mimics a real surface. *Faux*, the French word, means false or fake. So when you paint a faux finish on a furniture surface, you are out to fool a viewer into believing that the surface is made from leather, marble, wood or metal. The following four techniques will teach you how to turn a furniture surface into one that looks like it is made of either leather or marble or one that has developed patina through age, or verdigris (on metal surfaces).

You can create these techniques with a realistic look and develop a true faux finish or exaggerate the patterning of the technique to create more of a theatrical look. When working in larger interior spaces or commercial spaces, the theatrical look can be very effective. Experiment on different surfaces with these techniques. Each piece of furniture can yield a totally different finished effect even when the same exact technique is applied.

LEATHER LOOK

There is something so tactile about a leather surface. It is alluring to so many senses—touch, smell and sight. When I think of a leather surface, a masculine quality comes to mind. The leather look described here provides many of the qualities of real leather—texture, depth and dimension. Yet, by creating the painted illusion of leather, you can cover surfaces that normally would not be easily tooled in real leather.

A home office, a bedroom or a den seems a perfect place for the leather look technique to be applied to a variety of furniture surfaces. Classic finishes such as gilding complement the look of this leather technique.

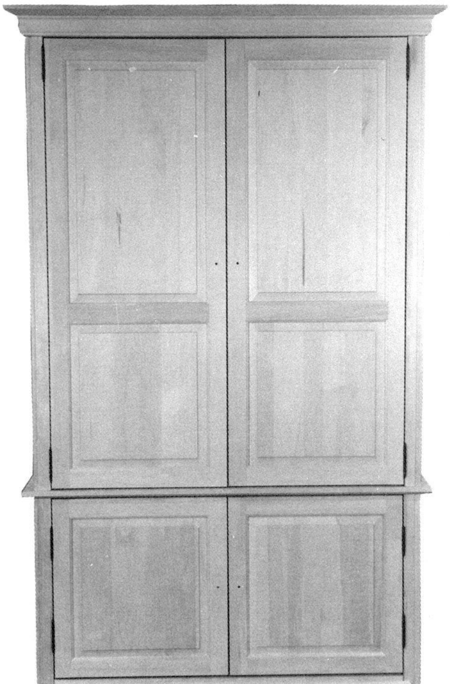

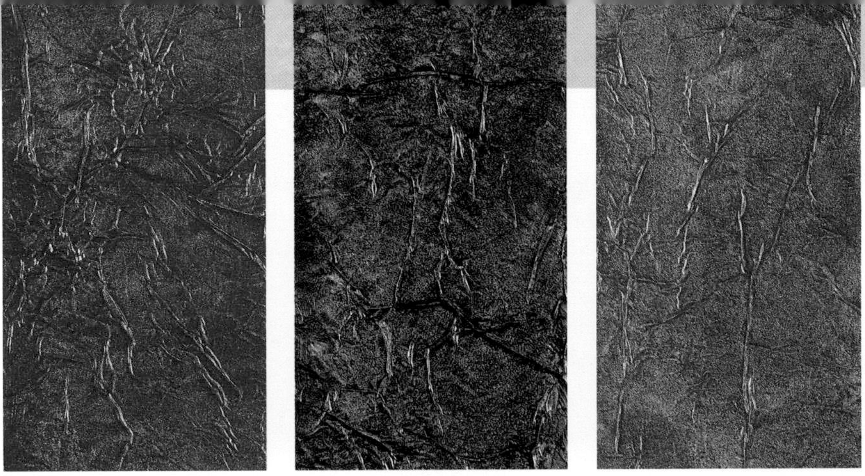

Optional color ways to create a leather look: right, Burnt Sienna plus Burnt Umber glaze over Cream base; center, Phthalo Green plus Raw Umber glaze over Cream base; left, Alizarin Crimson plus Burnt Umber over Cream base.

PREPARATION

Base coat the surface with a cream color (for light leather look) or black (for a dark leather look) in an acrylic or latex semigloss paint. Apply several coats until an opaque coverage is achieved. To achieve a smooth finish, you may need to sand lightly between coats with a fine grade of sandpaper. Let base coat thoroughly dry before proceeding. Prepare decoupage glue or thin white craft glue with water to a flowing consistency in a small container.

MATERIALS NEEDED:

- Paints—cream or black acrylic or latex semigloss; artist's acrylic colors in earth tone or chroma colors *(Sample project features Teal Green, Black and Alizarin Crimson plus Burnt Umber glaze)*
- Brushes—bristle base coat brush, glaze brush, varnish brush or 3-inch sponge brush
- Acrylic glazing medium
- White craft glue or decoupage glue
- Container—small tub
- Old toothbrush
- Brayer
- Kitchen sponge
- Bucket
- Tracing paper—artist's or draftsman's vellum
- Cotton rags
- Palette
- Palette knife
- Craft knife

Keys to Success

- Any imperfections in your base coat will show through to the topcoats. Take time to properly prepare the base coat.
- A wet sponge and bucket of water nearby can be a lifesaver when you need to quickly clean off excess glue or move the topcoat of tracing paper around the surface.
- You must seal the leather surface with several coats of varnish to protect the surface from tearing.

LEATHER LOOK

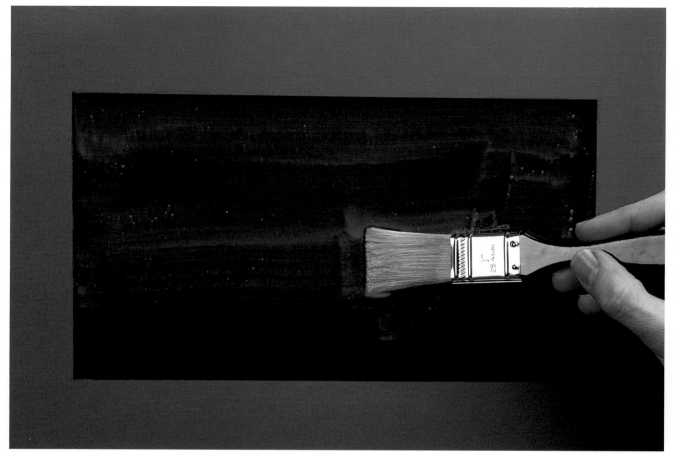

STEP 1. Lay several pieces of the tracing paper on the surface. You will work with slightly more square footage of tracing paper as compared to the surface to be covered. Now, crumple the individual sheets of tracing paper into a loose ball or wad. Smooth out the tracing paper. Dip inexpensive varnish or sponge brush in glue mixture, and coat the surface area to be covered in the leather look. Also, coat one side of a single smoothed out sheet of tracing paper. Apply generous coverage of glue to both surfaces. Any surface not covered with glue will not adhere properly.

STEP 2. Turn tracing paper over (glue side down), and adhere the paper to the surface by pressing the paper with your fingers. Smooth the paper out as much as you want. The more wrinkles in the paper, the more dimension in the finished leather look. Wipe down the surface with a moist kitchen sponge to remove excess glue. Roll over the surface with a brayer to remove any air bubbles. Let surface dry overnight. Cut excess away with sharp knife.

STEP 3. At this stage, you can lightly recoat the surface with the base coat color for a bold look or leave the transparent base color showing through the tracing paper and proceed with the next step—glazing (the latter looks great with a cream base coat and burnt umber glaze). If you choose to recoat the base color, brush on lightly with base coat brush. Don't allow heavy paint buildup to occur.

STEP 4. Make a transparent color tone glaze of clear acrylic glazing medium plus artist's acrylic color. Load glaze brush with color and stroke over surface. Work color into all crevasses. Wipe down surface with cotton rag to remove some of the top glaze color and to allow the base coat to show. Let the top glaze color collect into the crinkled pattern of the paper.

ANTIQUE LOOK

To antique means to age the piece of furniture through the use of tinted color glazes that create a haze over the surface. An antiqued finish is as if you were holding a tinted piece of acetate over the surface; you can still see down to the original surface color and decoration, but a transparent color has been cast over the surface. Antiquing, traditionally, is completed in dark earth tone colors, but as the furniture designer, you can break tradition and create antique glazes in any color.

The antiquing technique is well suited to be applied to any furniture surface for almost any setting in the home. Antiquing can be completed over a solid base coat color, or this technique could be executed over any of the other techniques found in this book.

PREPARATION

Base coat the surface in a semigloss acrylic or latex paint. Apply one coat and let dry. Sand the surface with a fine grade of sandpaper.

Optional color ways to create an antique look: right, White plus Payne's Gray antiquing over Phthalo Blue plus Black base; center, Black antiquing over Red Oxide base; left, Burnt Sienna plus Burnt Umber antiquing over Tan base.

Apply a second coat to achieve an opaque coverage. For interesting variations to the surface, you can base coat the surface with textured patterns. For a canvas or cross-weave pattern, base coat the surface in one direction, let dry, and then apply a second coat crossways. For extreme texture and random pattern, base coat the surface in a criss-cross style making overlapping X marks with your brush.

Keys to Success

- To achieve extreme texture in your base coat, use a very coarse hair brush to apply the paint and stroke it on in some type of pattern.
- To achieve an antiqued finish with a smooth color transition, your base coat must be sanded between coats to develop a glasslike surface.
- The cloth you use to wipe the surface can leave marks in the antique color glaze. This can be desirable or undesirable. Panty hose or 100 percent cotton cloth leaves the least marks, cheesecloth leaves some marks, and tarlatan leaves the most marks.
- You can vary the degree of transparency of the glaze by adding more color or acrylic glaze.
- On larger pieces of furniture, you want to work on one panel or section at a time to allow adequate open time of the acrylic glaze.

ANTIQUE LOOK

STEP 1. Create the antiquing mixture by mixing artist's acrylic color(s) with the acrylic glazing medium. The antiquing glaze should be a flowing, soupy consistency with no visible lumps of paint. Test the level of paint transparency by rubbing a little color glaze on the surface. Adjust the glaze accordingly. Load the glaze brush with antiquing glaze, and brush over surface. Be sure to work glaze into all recesses of the piece (molding, carved section).

STEP 2. Wad up cloth in your hand. Remove some of the antiquing glaze in central areas of the furniture piece. When wiping, follow the natural direction of the surface (horizontal for tops and drawers, vertical for legs and sides). Remove as little or as much color as you desire. Let antiquing stay darker in the recessed areas.

STEP 3. To soften the transition between the darker and lighter areas, use the mop brush to blend. Holding the brush in an upright manner, lightly dust the surface back and forth until you see the paint begin to move. Do not apply heavy pressure on the brush; that would only remove paint. Your goal is to make a soft, gradual transition between the contrasting areas of the antiquing glaze.

STEP 4. To soften the variations in color value from dark to light, especially when antiquing with bright and intense colors, a "ghost" antiquing glaze (very transparent glaze) can be added to the surface. Let the first antiquing glaze dry, then mix a transparent inklike-consistency color and brush it over the surface with the glaze brush. While second glaze is still wet, run over the glaze with the flogger brush. Use the mop brush to blend and soften into the antiquing coloration that already exists. Flyspecking can be added for extra interest.

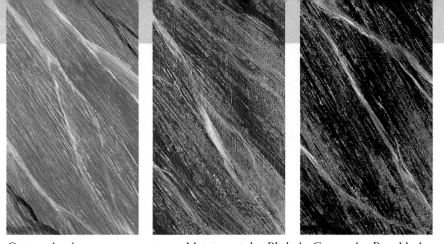

Optional color ways to create marbleizing: right, Phthalo Green plus Raw Umber glaze over Cream base with white and black veins; center, Burnt Sienna glaze over Cream with white and Burnt Umber veins; left, white plus Payne's Gray glaze over Cream with white and black veins.

MARBLEIZING

The most popular of all faux finishes is marbleizing. To be able to duplicate the look of real marble through the use of paint and brush is quite special. For every type of marble, there is a method to duplicate it through painted finishes. The marble pattern taught here is a fractured pattern completed in a pink-rose tone. The name of this marble is Rose Aurora. This technique can be applied with any color you desire, so if rose tones don't fit your decor, simply alter the palette of colors.

Marbleizing can be applied to virtually any surface—furniture, accessories, walls, ceilings and floors. To make the painted marble look as real as possible, you must consider how the real surface would be installed or built. On interior surfaces, such as floors and walls, marble would be installed in a tile or panel pattern. On some larger pieces of furniture, the marble or several types of marbles may be sectioned off into an inlaid pattern. Marbleizing can become very pattern active on a piece of furniture, so simple, understated techniques, such as pickling, gel staining and antiquing, can be used to complement the painted marble.

PREPARATION

Base coat the surface with a semigloss acrylic or latex paint in a cream tone. Apply one coat and let dry. Sand the surface with a fine grade of sandpaper, and remove sanding dust with tack rag. Recoat the surface until an opaque coverage is achieved. Open several sheets of newspaper to their fullest opening. Now, fold vertically in an accordion style (the whole length of the sheet). The folds should be about one inch wide. Now, fold this long accordion piece of paper in half.

MATERIALS NEEDED:
- Paints—cream acrylic or latex semigloss; artist's acrylic colors (*Sample project features Ecru base coat, Raw Umber, Alizarin Crimson, Burnt Umber, Titanium White*)
- Brushes—bristle base coat brush, glaze brush, blending softener brush, mop brush
- Acrylic glazing medium
- Container—small tub
- Fine-pointed chicken feathers
- Old toothbrush
- Cotton rags
- Newspaper
- Rubbing alcohol
- Palette
- Palette knife

Keys to Success
* The vein structure of the painted marble should be executed following a few principles: Painted veins should not intersect forming an X; veins do not branch out in multipatterns like tree branches; veins should shift from different diagonals on the same plane.
* To develop the feeling of fossilized layers, paint and patterning must be added and then partially subtracted to expose the layer below.
* For a realistic look when working with large areas, the surface must be divided into sections or tilelike marble patterns. Paint each one individually with alternating veining directions.
* When creating the fossilized pattern, if you wait too long and the paint has set up and begun to dry, no paint reaction will occur with the rubbing alcohol.

MARBLEIZING

STEP 1. Make a dark value burnt rose color from Alizarin Crimson plus Raw Umber plus Burnt Umber (60:30:10 ratio). Starting with a pile of Titanium White, slowly add the dark rose mixture to it, continually mixing the colors thoroughly with the palette knife to achieve a midvalue burnt rose. Place paint in a container and add acrylic glaze medium until a thin, soupy, transparent consistency is mixed. Brush color glaze over marble section.

STEP 2. Hit the surface with the folded edge of the newspaper. Create a diagonal pattern of "fractured" marks. To create contrast, hit the surface harder in some areas to remove more color, and create lighter areas with softer hits. To create a fossilized pattern, dip a toothbrush in rubbing alcohol and flyspeck the surface. Where the alcohol hits the surface, a chemical reaction will occur forcing the paint away and leaving spotted, colored rings. Let dry.

STEP 3. Thin the rose glaze with more acrylic glazing medium for a greater transparency (inklike). Brush over surface. To develop the first layer of veins, load the tip of the feather in an inklike-consistency mixture of Raw Umber plus acrylic glazing medium. Holding the feather like a violin bow, stroke the feather's tip and side across the wet surface. The vein should softly fade away in areas and get slightly bolder in others. Soften veins by dusting with a blending softener brush and mop brush. Let dry.

STEP 4. Recoat the surface with the transparent rose glaze. Load a clean feather with Titanium White that has been thinned to an inklike consistency with acrylic glazing medium. Stroke the feather's tip and side along the surface making ragged diagonal marks. The white veins should be more dominant than the Raw Umber veins. Set the veins into the surface by brushing over them with the blending softener brush. Flyspeck the surface with Raw Umber and then rubbing alcohol for paint reaction. Let dry. An overglaze of transparent rose can be placed over the entire surface to soften vein markings, if necessary.

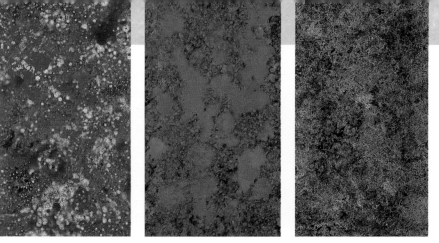

PATINA VERDIGRIS

A painted verdigris finish mimics the green patina or crust of copper sulfate that forms on copper, brass and bronze exposed to air or sea water for a long period of time. The technique to create this look can be built up slowly to establish a soft verdigris, or it can be multilayered to establish an aged look. Because the coloration can catch and collect in the dimensional areas, surfaces best suited for this technique are ones with carved or recessed areas of texture.

Rooms with garden themes, such as a breakfast room, patio, solarium or sun room, are excellent places in the home to design with a patina verdigris finish. Furniture and accessories with dimensional qualities will display this technique at its best.

Optional color ways to create patina finishes: right, Gold base with Pewter Black darkening solution; center, Copper base with Patina Blue solution; left, Gold base with English Brown darkening solution.

PREPARATION

Prime the surface to seal and protect. Base coat the surface with a couple of coats of black in an acrylic or latex semigloss paint. This dark value provides a solid background for the copper to be placed over. Sand lightly between coats. Let base coat thoroughly dry before proceeding.

MATERIALS NEEDED:

- Paints—Copper Topper and Patina Green solutions; black acrylic or latex semigloss
- Brush—bristle base coat brush
- Containers—two small tubs
- Paint stir
- Sea sponge
- Plastic gloves
- Spray mister bottle (optional)
- Old toothbrush (optional)

Keys to Success

❋ If you don't achieve the look you desire on the first series of color and chemical applications, continue to build up additional layers.

❋ On surfaces to be viewed vertically, allow copper and chemicals to run down the surface to create a realistic look.

❋ The copper must be applied over a sealed, semigloss surface for best results.

❋ For a spotted or pitted look, pour chemical into spray mister bottle and spritz surface.

PATINA VERDIGRIS

STEP 1. Stipple on the base coat of black with the base coat bristle brush. To stipple, you'll lightly hit the surface with the tip end of the bristles. Let dry and recoat. Thoroughly stir the Copper Topper and Patina Green bottles. Pour some Copper Topper into tub.

STEP 2. Using the base coat bristle brush, apply Copper Topper to surface. Apply copper in random crisscross strokes. Stipple on the Copper Topper to place copper into crevasses. Allow first coat of Copper Topper to dry.

STEP 3. Apply a second coat of copper to the surface in the same manner as Step 1. While the coating of copper is still wet, pour the Patina Green solution into another tub. Wearing plastic gloves and using a clean sea sponge, coat Patina Green over wet copper. Coat by randomly hitting the surface with the sponge and allowing some of the copper to remain uncoated with Patina Green. Let dry to determine how the pattern of the chemical reaction will appear.

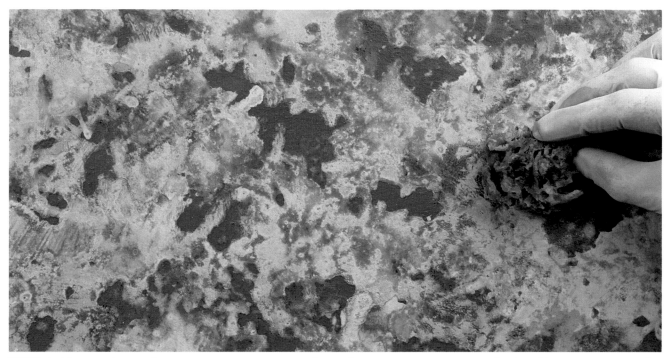

STEP 4. Now, evaluate where you want more green and straight copper areas to appear. Apply additional copper, and then cover with Patina Green for verdigris look. Note, some areas may simply need additional washes of copper. For a pitted look of verdigris, brush on copper and then fill spray mister bottle with Patina Green and spritz the surface for reaction.

CHAPTER 5
TEXTURE TECHNIQUES

Crackled Finish
Distressed Finish
Foil Gilding
Torn Paper

Texture can add a great deal of interest to a piece of furniture. These techniques provide a tactile quality to the surface, providing a level of fascination to the viewer. You'll want to run your fingers over these surfaces; they simply call out to be touched and felt. Three of the four techniques provide dimensional texture—crackled finish, distressed finish and torn paper—while foil gilding provides a visual texture quality.

Follow these instructions for a good foundation, but don't be afraid to experiment with different color combinations. Practice on sample boards to develop the right combination of technique and color for your piece of furniture.

CRACKLED FINISH

A paint finish that duplicates a crackled look is imitating what happens naturally when one incompatible product is placed over another. Through time, a crackled, or crazed, pattern of fine or large cracks appears on the surface; this occurs because one product is actually fighting with the other, and there is a lack of proper breathing space and adhesion that develops on the surface. Temperature and weather conditions can also affect a surface, thus creating a natural crackled finish. To create this pattern on purpose, instead of by accident, you'll cause your own chemical reaction.

All types of furniture from traditional to modern can look great with a crackled finish applied to them. Accessories from lamps to small boxes are perfect to receive this finish. Walls can also be completed with the crackled finish, al-

Optional color ways to create a crackle finish: right, White base with Green antiquing over crackle finish; center, Red Oxide base with Black antiquing over crackle finish; left, Yellow base with Burnt Umber antiquing over crackle finish.

though this application can be quite time-consuming on such a massive surface.

PREPARATION

Prime and seal the surface. Choose desired base coat color, and apply several coats to achieve an opaque coverage. If you wish to place a crackled finish over any design or patterned work—stenciling, decorative painting or faux finish—complete that work first. Allow base paints to thoroughly dry before proceeding.

MATERIALS NEEDED:
- Paints—desired base color in acrylic or latex semigloss; artist's acrylic colors (*Sample project features Sand base coat, Dark Brown glaze*)
- Brushes—base coat bristle brush, varnish brush, glaze brush, mop brush
- Acrylic glazing medium
- Water base polyurethane varnish
- Oil base polyurethane varnish
- Container—small tub
- Turpentine
- Cotton rags
- Palette
- Palette knife
- Paint stirs
- Old toothbrush (optional)

Keys to Success

❦ Timing is the most critical aspect to this technique. If you wait too long between layering of products, the desired crackled finish will not appear or only will appear in some areas.

❦ Constantly test the surface after Step 1 to see if the surface has reached its tacky state. Touch surface lightly with finger.

❦ A thin coating of both products will yield the best results.

❦ Always brush every coat on the surface in the same direction.

CRACKLED FINISH

STEP 1. Gently stir oil base varnish with paint stir. Load the varnish brush with oil base polyurethane and coat the surface. Brush on a smooth, flowing coat of varnish, but use caution not to create a massive buildup of varnish on the surface. Let the varnish begin to dry. You need to let the varnish reach its tacky state, which, depending on environments, can be anywhere from fifteen to twenty-five minutes. Test often, by placing a finger on the surface, to see if surface has reached the tacky state. If your finger sticks and receives slight resistance and the surface feels like sticky honey, you are ready to proceed.

STEP 2. Stir the water base varnish slowly with paint stir so you don't cause an excessive amount of air bubbles to form in the container. Using a clean varnish brush, apply an even, thin coating of water base varnish over the tacky oil base varnish. Be careful not to apply the varnish too dryly or too heavily. The crackled pattern will not occur satisfactorily if this coating is not completed correctly. Allow varnish coatings to dry overnight. As the two coatings dry at different rates, the crackled pattern will start to form.

STEP 3. After the surface is thoroughly cured and the crackled pattern has formed, you'll want to magnify the patterning by overglazing or antiquing the surface. This glazing can be completed in a range of colors depending on the desired effect. Earth tone glazing will furnish an aged look, bright color tone glazing will yield a bold look, and subtle tone glazing will create a decorator look. Mix chosen acrylic color with acrylic glazing medium to transparent, flowing, soupy consistency. Brush on surface with glaze brush in a scrubbing motion.

STEP 4. Crumple cotton rag in your hand. Begin wiping excess glaze off surface, allowing the color glaze to catch in the crackled pattern. For added interest to the piece, wipe off additional glaze in any areas you wish to create a highlight. For contrast, add more glaze by dipping your fingertip in color and rubbing it on the surface. Soften extra coloring into surface by color glazing and flyspecking onto the surface.

DISTRESSED FINISH

A distressed finish is one that shows signs of being marred and literally beat up over time. The goal is to depict the surface as if it had been aged through misuse. You can take this technique to many different levels, from a very subtle look to an extreme distressing—as if the piece had been dragged behind a truck. Wood surfaces are best suited for the distressed technique, but metal surfaces could also be distressed.

Casual rooms and furniture are the natural choices for this technique. Kitchens, dens and family rooms are ideal locations for distressed furniture and accessories. When completing distressing, you may want to consider the addition of antiquing, due to the fact that the two techniques tend to go hand in hand.

Optional color ways to create a distressed finish: right, Tan base with distressing and Burnt Umber antiquing; center, Black on first coat and Gold on second coat with distressing and black antiquing; left, Light Green first coat and Dark Green second coat with distressing.

PREPARATION

Prime the surface to seal and protect. Base coat the surface with a couple coats of acrylic or latex flat paint. Note, you can apply several layers of different colors. Hints of these various colors will show up as you begin to distress the surface. Let base coat thoroughly dry before proceeding.

MATERIALS NEEDED:

- Paints—desired base color in acrylic or latex flat; artist's acrylic colors (*Sample project features Goldenrod base coat, Eggshell glaze*)
- Brushes—bristle base coat brush, glaze brush, mop brush
- Acrylic glazing medium
- Sandpaper—several grits from coarse to fine
- Tools—hammer, screwdriver, screws, nails, chain
- Container—small tub
- Cotton rags
- Palette
- Palette knife
- Old toothbrush (optional)

Keys to Success

❋ Be sure to apply a flat paint to the surface. A satin, semigloss or gloss paint will not sand off as well and will not leave interesting distress marks.

❋ If you are unsure what level of distressing to complete, build slowly and take off sections of the base coat one at a time.

❋ To soften the look of distressing, apply overglazing or antiquing to the surface.

❋ Be sure you want to distress a piece before beginning. It is very time-consuming and in some cases impossible to undo this technique.

DISTRESSED FINISH

STEP 1. Using a medium grade of sandpaper, lightly sand the surface to remove the top layers of paint. If you have layered the surface with several colors, you'll want to proceed slowly in the distressing process in order for each layer of color to be exposed in certain areas. Be sure to sand in the areas of the surface where the paint would naturally wear, such as furniture edges, corners, legs and arms.

STEP 2. To develop stronger areas of distress, begin using a coarse sandpaper on the surface. Allow scratches from the sandpaper to form, as well as gouged areas. Develop transition between coarse and light distressed areas by using the medium to fine sandpaper to create midtone levels of distressing.

STEP 3. For a stronger quality of distressing, randomly hit the surface with a hammer to create dents. Nails and screws will leave interesting marks by scratching with their tips or laying them on their sides and hitting them with the hammer. A metal chain can also leave marks and patterns by hitting the surface.

STEP 4. To highlight the distressing, make a transparent glaze with acrylic colors and acrylic glazing medium. Brush glaze on surface, and wipe off excess with cotton rag. The glaze will collect and catch in the recessed areas of the distressing. Soften any areas of the glazing by blending with the mop brush. For added interest, flyspeck the surface with a toothbrush loaded with color glaze.

FOIL GILDING

There is no easier way to achieve the rich qualities of the addition of a gold-leaf-like finish to a surface than with foil gilding. You can try to substitute with metallic paints, but the finished look does not achieve the same results as the addition of the foil to a surface. Foil leaf is available in gold, silver and copper. Foil gilding can be completed as a trim element, to create a design element, or to totally engulf a surface.

This technique will create an elegant look and is best suited for application on furniture to be used in formal settings, such as living and dining rooms. Smaller accessories of candle followers, obelisks, corbels, drapery rods and rings are perfect surfaces to receive foil leaf.

PREPARATION

Prime and seal the surface. Base the area to be gilded in the appropriate background color: Under gold foil, base coat in Red Oxide; under silver foil, base coat in Payne's Gray plus white (midtone); under copper foil, base coat in Burnt Sienna. Apply several coats of base color until opaque. Sand lightly between each coat to achieve a smooth finish. Brush on a coat of water base varnish to seal the surface.

Optional color ways to create gilding: right, gray base with silver foil and Payne's Gray antiquing; center, black base with red foil and black antiquing; left, Burnt Sienna base with copper foil and Burnt Umber antiquing.

MATERIALS NEEDED:
- Paints—desired base coat in artist's acrylic colors (depending on type of leaf to be applied) of Red Oxide, Payne's Gray, Titanium White or Burnt Sienna; or Mars Black or Burnt Umber for antiquing gilded areas (*Sample project features Red Oxide base coat, Black glaze*)
- Brushes—bristle base coat brush, sponge brush, no. 3 round golden natural, mop brush
- Acrylic glazing medium
- Foil sizing or adhesive
- Cotton rags
- Burnishing tool
- Tracing paper—one 8½" × 11" piece

Keys to Success

❋ The surface to be gilded must be as smooth as possible. Any imperfections in the base coat will be magnified when the foil leaf is placed over the surface. A glasslike smoothness will yield the best finished result.

❋ Be sure to follow the instructions on the setup time of the sizing. There is a window of working time when the foil will adhere to the sizing. Once you go beyond that time period, the foil will not properly stick to the surface.

❋ Take time when you burnish the surface; if the foil does not get rubbed down to the surface, it will not stay.

❋ Take care in handling the foil; placing the clear carrier sheet on the adhesive will tend to pull up the adhesive.

FOIL GILDING

STEP 1. Brush on an even, flowing coat of foil sizing to all areas to which you wish the gold to adhere. Note that where sizing is coated on the surface is where the foil will stick. So if you mistakenly get any sizing on surrounding areas, quickly wipe and clean away. Following the sizing label's instructions, allow the sizing to reach its tacky state. This can be anywhere from sixty minutes to two hours or longer.

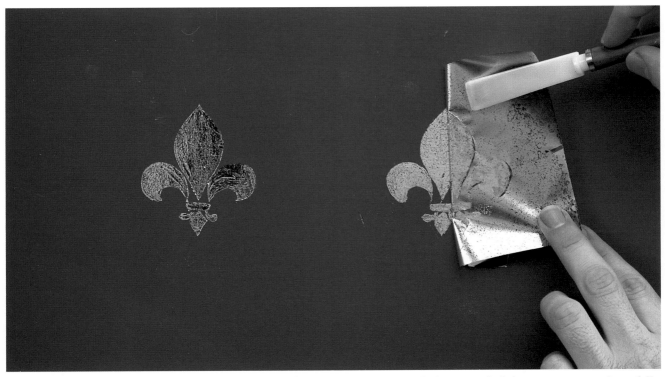

STEP 2. Cut foil sheets to a size slightly larger than the area to be covered. Pick up one foil sheet at a time, and carefully place foil on the sized areas. With the clear plastic carrier sheet on top, burnish over the foil with a burnishing tool. To create an overall gilded look, you'll want to overlap each piece of foil. If you want to create a worn, antique look, you can leave small- to medium-size separations between foil applications. Allow sizing with foil to dry overnight before proceeding

STEP 3. Create an antiquing glaze to tone down the brightness of the gold foil. Mix black or earth tone colors with acrylic glazing medium to develop a transparent, soupy glaze. Brush over surface with glaze brush. Be sure to work glaze into recessed areas, such as molding and trim.

STEP 4. Remove antiquing glaze by rubbing the surface with a cotton rag. Be sure to wipe out highlights near and around the gilded areas. If too much is removed and gold foil seems too strong again, add overglaze and soften. For interest, add flyspecking; load a toothbrush with glaze, and run your thumb over bristles to cause paint flecks to hit surface.

TORN PAPER

The torn paper technique can add a great deal of texture to a surface. In some color combinations, the torn paper technique can begin to take on a leather look. This technique also allows you to develop tone-on-tone looks all the way to very high contrast, bold effects. You'll be layering the paper, one piece over another, so a good deal of dimension will be built up on the furniture surface.

The finished effect yields a modern approach, so an interior environment that can be designed with contemporary furniture or an eclectic mix will be best suited for the torn paper technique. Furniture and larger accessories can be covered with the paper.

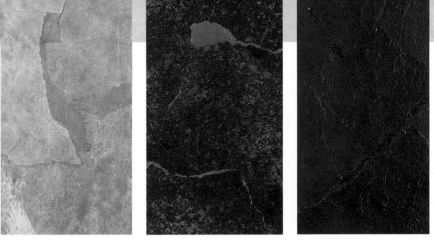

Optional color ways to create a torn paper look: right, Red Oxide base with Black glaze; center, sponging with three shades of green; left, Cream base with Pink glaze ragged off.

PREPARATION

Prime and seal surface to receive torn paper. Base coat panels of paper in desired color. Complete any faux finish technique you wish to apply to the painted paper panels, such as glazing, ragging or texturizing (paper shown received two-tone glazing). Allow to dry.

MATERIALS NEEDED:
- Paints—desired base color in acrylic or latex semigloss; artist's acrylic colors (*Sample project features Ecru base coat, Pale Pink glaze*)
- Brushes—bristle base coat brush, glaze brush
- Acrylic glazing medium
- Water base varnish
- Brown paper sacks or roll of sheathing paper cut into panels
- Wallpaper paste—heavy-duty
- Kitchen sponge
- Wallpaper brush
- Brayer
- Bucket
- Mat knife with sharp blade

Keys to Success
✳ Be sure to prepare enough base-coated panels to cover the desired surface. You'll need about one and one-half times more paper coverage in solid sheet form to cover the surface once paper is torn into pieces.

✳ For a tone-on-tone look, glaze torn edges the same color as base coat. For high contrast, glaze torn edges in contrasting colors.

✳ Be sure to smooth out each piece of torn paper as you adhere it to the surface. Roll excess glue from underneath paper with brayer.

✳ Avoid surfaces with carved or recessed areas that would be difficult to work paper around.

TORN PAPER

STEP 1. Tear painted paper in random pieces. Scale torn paper pieces to the proportion of the furniture piece. Mix desired color tone with acrylic glazing medium, and brush on torn edges. Complete this step on all pieces and allow to dry.

STEP 2. Coat the back of several torn pieces of paper with heavy-duty wallpaper paste. Pick up one piece at a time, and randomly lay on surface. Smooth piece out with a moist kitchen sponge, and then brush over with wallpaper brush. Run brayer over paper with a good deal of pressure to remove excess glue under paper. Clean glue away with sponge.

STEP 3. Pick up the next piece of paper, and overlap a part of it on the surrounding pieces. Clean with sponge, brush with wallpaper brush and stroke with brayer. Once larger area is complete, go back and thoroughly clean sponge in a bucket of water and wipe down surface. It is important to remove all traces of excess glue.

STEP 4. Skip around surface when you apply pieces so a natural, random pattern is developed. Trim excess pieces that go beyond surface with a sharp craft knife. After all pieces are in place, allow surface to dry several days. Protect paper with several coats of water base varnish.

CHAPTER 6
PATTERNING TECHNIQUES

Stenciling
Striping
Mosaic
Design Presses

The addition of pattern and design to a surface creates a great deal of interest to the furniture surface. Designs that you create and apply to a piece of furniture allow you to tie in the subject matter that exists on the other elements of your interior. Wallpaper, fabric and carpet designs can easily be transferred in part or whole to the work you complete on furniture and will develop a custom one-of-a-kind look to your home. In this chapter, four pattern, or design, techniques are covered, each one providing a different approach.

Two of the techniques—stenciling and design presses—establish subject matter designs, while the other two techniques—striping and mosaic—create graphic patterns. A key to keep in mind when designing with these various patterns: Use great care with multiple patterns in a room. You can easily create a room where a "pattern fight" will occur. Keep multiple patterns to a minimum, and let one be the dominant focus with brightness of color and weight of pattern.

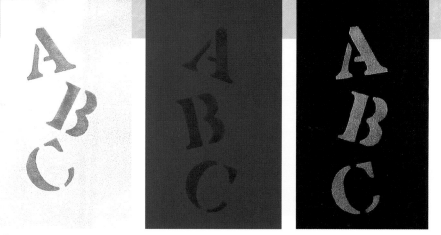

STENCILING

Stenciling is one of the quickest and easiest ways to repeat a decorative pattern on a furniture or accessory piece. To stencil means to apply color through a cut opening on a piece of acetate or Mylar plastic. You can stencil in several different styles from opaque to shaded. You can also use different tools to apply the color—brush, sponge or spray.

Casual rooms are best suited for stenciled patterns, although in the Victorian era, extremely elaborate stencils were used in formal living and dining room settings. Children's theme projects are ideally suited for stencil designs due to the fact that this technique can create a childlike cutout look.

PREPARATION

Prepare new or old wood following standard procedures. Prime and base coat the surface to be stenciled with a flat acrylic or latex paint. Sand lightly between coats to achieve a smooth finish. Remove sanding dust with a tack rag. Use commercially made stencils or cut your own stencil from a Mylar plastic sheet using a stencil burning tool or craft knife, a pattern, and a sheet of glass. Place glass over the pattern design, and tape Mylar over glass. Use craft knife to cut or stencil burner to burn through plastic. Cut a separate stencil overlay for each section of the design where different colors are within one inch of

Optional color ways to use stenciling: right, Gold stenciling over Black base; center, Burnt Umber stenciling over Burnt Sienna base; left, Cerulean Blue plus White stenciling over White base.

each other. On each overlay, use a permanent black marker to create guidelines (dotted marks) to use as you stencil to line up the overlay with the previously completed section.

MATERIALS NEEDED:
- Paints—desired base color in acrylic or latex flat; artist's acrylic colors (*Sample project features white flat latex base coat, Cadmium Yellow Light, Burnt Sienna, Cadmium Red Medium, Phthalo Green, Cobalt Blue and Mars Black*)
- Brushes—stencil brushes in a variety of sizes, script liner brush
- Precut stencils (or make your own with sheets of clear Mylar, designs, a sheet of glass, craft knife or stencil burner tool, and permanent fine line marker)
- Repositionable tape
- Natural sea sponge (optional)
- Paper towels

Keys to Success
❀ Be sure to base coat the surface to be stenciled with a flat paint. Satin, semigloss and gloss base coat paints will be too slick, and as you stencil, the paint will tend to smear.
❀ Gradually build up color on a section of the stencil. This will allow you to shade and create various values within the stenciled object.
❀ Excessive pressure on the stencil brush, sponge or spray nozzle will cause paint to bleed under the stencil and create messy looking paint edges.
❀ For simple stencil overlays, you can create all shading in one step. For more elaborate stencil overlays, complete one level of color at a time at each place the pattern repeats, and then return to the starting point to develop stronger values or to add detail.

STENCILING

STEP 1. Load the stencil brush by lightly dabbing the bristle tips in color. Using a circular motion, dry wipe some excess color off on a paper towel. Move brush over to stencil that has been taped into position, and place the brush on the stencil cutout's edge. Lay the bristle of the brush half on the open surface and half on the plastic surface. Using a light circular motion, dust the color on the perimeter of the stencil.

STEP 2. Go over major areas with one pass of color. Place stronger amounts of color on the outside edge of the subject. Be sure to leave a highlight on some objects to create a dimensional quality to the subject matter. (Optional: For a more casual to coarse look, apply color with a small piece of a natural sea sponge.)

STENCILING

STEP 3. Some parts of your stencil design will need a third pass of color placed on the edge of the design for stronger contrast and dimension building. To direct this specific color placement, place about one eighth of the stencil brush's bristles into the opening and let the remaining bristles lie on the plastic. You'll need to hold the stencil firmly to direct the darker value exactly where you want it placed. Brush on color in a circular motion.

STEP 4. In some cases, your stencil design may require additional detail work. You can add interest to the stencil by adding vein lines, branches, facial features and decorative accents. To create this work, thin desired detailing color with water. The paint should be thinned down to an inklike consistency. Load a script liner brush with color, and using the tip of the brush, stroke on detailing. Use a light touch on brush to prevent a heavy look to this work.

STRIPING

Striping has become one of the more popular decorative treatments you can apply to your interiors. As the name of the technique implies, you'll create a series of stripes—opaque or tonal in either horizontal or vertical directions or a combination of both. You can complete striping in various tones of the same color (for a soft tone-on-tone look) or use various colors (for a more active, contrasting pattern).

Depending on the stripe itself, you can create anything from a very elegant look to a country look. The striping technique will fit into any room of the home and almost any decor style.

PREPARATION

Prime and seal the surface. Choose desired base coat color in semigloss, and apply several coats to achieve an opaque coverage. Sand lightly between coats, and remove dust with tack rag to achieve a smooth base coating.

Optional color ways to use striping: right, Forest Green base with Leaf Green stripes; center, Goldenrod base with sponged Metallic Gold stripes; left, Sand base with White glazed stripes.

MATERIALS NEEDED:
- Paints—desired base color in acrylic or latex semigloss (*Sample project features Edgewater Blue and Dark Williamsburg*)
- Brushes—base coat bristle brush, glaze brush, flogger brush, no. 16 golden natural flat brush
- Acrylic glazing medium
- Water base polyurethane varnish
- Pencils
- Ruler
- Repositionable tape
- Burnishing tool

Keys to Success
- ❋ If you do not take the proper time to burnish the tape properly, paint bleeding will occur under the tape's edge.
- ❋ If the surface is not properly prepared through sanding, priming and base coating, the tape can pull up all previous layers down to the substratum.
- ❋ Be sure to use repositionable tape, which can be easily pulled off the surface. Some masking tape's strong adhesive will pull up base coats down to the substratum.
- ❋ Always brush along the tape's edge; don't brush into the tape's edge. The latter will force paint to seep under tape.

STRIPING

STEP 1. Mark off desired stripe pattern—a series of horizontal or vertical stripes or a combination of both. Take your time to mark off the surface carefully. Any misplaced marks will be magnified when painted. Use a light touch when marking the lines. This will prevent indentations from forming on the surface.

STEP 2. Apply strips of tape to the surface following the pencil guidelines. Place tape just outside of the pencil line so the paint will cover the pencil work. Using a burnishing tool, rub down the edge(s) of tape where paint will be brushed. It is not necessary to burnish the entire width of the tape (this will cause difficulty in removing tape later).

STEP 3. Determine if you want to paint the stripe with solid color or create a pattern into a wet paint glaze. If you prefer the latter, mix a transparent paint glaze (thin, creamy consistency) with color and acrylic glazing medium. Brush color glaze on stripe with glaze brush, and make marks into the wet glaze. Here, the flogger brush is dragged down the stripe of wet paint to create a strie pattern. Let dry.

STEP 4. To create a horizontal and vertical pattern, repeat Steps 2 and 3 in the opposite direction. Let dry. For a plaid quality to the stripes, tape off intersection area and brush on a darker glaze. Use the no. 16 golden natural flat brush to stroke on a loose, cross-weave pattern. Remove tape and allow to dry.

MOSAIC

A mosaic is simply a decorative design made from small pieces of colored tile or colored glass (tessera) that are set into mortar. You can create a mosaic pattern of graphic, geometric designs, free-form designs, or designs made of specific subject matter. A mosaic pattern is often quite loose in its grid structure of the individual pieces placed in the mortar. Unlike the tile pattern of the installation of your kitchen or bathroom, where the tile lines up in a perfect parallel grid, mosaic grids are less rigid.

The type of furniture or accessory piece you place the mosaic pattern on will determine in what style of room it will best be displayed. A tabletop with a mosaic pattern looks great in a garden room, porch or sun room. An elegant accessory box can be a dynamic design for a formal living room.

PREPARATION

Prime and seal the surface. Base coat the area that will receive the mosaic pattern; use a putty-colored gray tone. Use a flat acrylic or latex base paint and the base coat bristle brush. Apply several coats until an opaque coverage is achieved. Sand lightly between coats, and remove sanding dust with a tack rag. Mark off desired grid structure with pencil and ruler. These will only be rough guidelines to follow.

Optional color ways to create a mosaic look: right, Black base with White tile shapes and Payne's Gray antiquing; center, Sand base with Green, Blue and Yellow tile shapes and Burnt Umber antiquing; left, Sky Blue base with White tile shapes and Black antiquing.

MATERIALS NEEDED:

- Paints—desired base color in acrylic or latex flat; artist's acrylic colors (*Sample project features Mushroom base coat, Yellow Ochre, Burnt Sienna, Indian Brown glaze*)
- Brushes—base coat bristle brush, glaze brush, varnish brush, mop brush
- Acrylic glazing medium
- Water base polyurethane varnish
- Cotton rags
- Palette
- Palette knife
- Craft knife
- Pencil
- Ruler
- Foam panels
- Hot glue gun and glue sticks

Keys to Success

✽ A geometric graphic design will be the easiest design to start off with on your first project. The guidelines will provide you with a framework to work within and create structure.

✽ Cut out different tile shapes. Using the same size tile will cause a tight, controlled design to form; it will create a kitchen tile look.

✽ Be sure to use different colors to divide sections of the graphic pattern. When creating a subject matter such as a leaf or flower design, use different values of the same color within the subject to create dimension.

MOSAIC

STEP 1. Cut strips of foam with a ruler and craft knife. Cut strips into various lengths to make the tiles: ½″, ¾″, 1″ and 1½″. Create handles about 5 inches long. Hot glue foam tile pieces to foam handle pieces. Thin acrylic colors with acrylic glazing medium to a thin, creamy consistency. Load tile end in paint and stamp on palette to coat foam evenly. Touch furniture surface following marked guidelines. Create perimeter of one section.

STEP 2. Now, work within the perimeter of the shape outlined. Create a row at a time, alternating between both sides of the perimeter. You can be loose and free with the tile placement. Use smaller pieces to fit into the spaces that remain open. You can vary the values of the color that you are working with by touching the surface several times before reloading the tile foam.

STEP 3. After the tile design has been stamped out and is dry, you'll want to tone down the tiles to make it appear that they are set into the mortar. Create a transparent color glaze with a dark color such as an earth tone or black hue. Thin color with acrylic glazing medium to an inklike consistency. Brush on with a glaze brush.

STEP 4. Wipe away excess glaze with a cotton rag. Be sure to buff out highlight areas in the center of the surface for more interest. Smooth out color glaze by lightly dusting the surface with a mop brush. If you wish to create a more rugged look, you can hit the surface with a sea sponge moistened with water. The damp sponge will cause a pitted look on the tile and mortar.

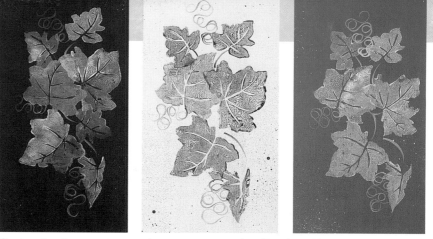

DESIGN PRESSES

The design press technique is similar to creating stamp designs on a surface, but instead of loading a rubber stamp on an ink pad, you'll load a design cut from a dense foam pad with paint by stroking color across the bottom of the design pad. The result will be repetitive design elements that have a relaxed feel. The design presses can be placed on a surface in a free-form layout, a border layout or a centralized layout. Detail can be added to the design by using a permanent marker or script liner brush.

Furniture pieces to be placed in the kitchen, bedroom, bathroom or family room are perfect for the casual look of the design presses. This technique also translates ideally to wall, ceiling and floor surfaces.

PREPARATION

Prime and seal the piece of furniture. Base coat the surface areas to receive the design presses with a flat acrylic or latex paint. Brush on several smooth coats of paint using the base coat bristle brushes until an opaque coverage is achieved. Sand lightly between coats removing sanding dust with a tack rag. Use commercially made design presses, or cut your own from dense foam. Tape all edges of your design to the foam. Using a sharp blade on a craft knife, cut the design out of foam. Create a small tab on the side to

Optional color ways to use design presses: right, Cerulean Blue base with White and Light Blue glaze leaves; center, Sand base with Burnt Sienna and Burnt Umber glaze leaves; left, Leaf Green base with Light Green and White glaze leaves.

hold the design press. Cut inner detail, such as leaf veins, by lightly scoring the center of the foam. Cut a fine line in the foam to create detail in the shape, if desired, such as the center vein of the leaf shown.

MATERIALS NEEDED:

- Paints—desired base color in acrylic or latex flat; artist's acrylic colors (*Sample project features white flat latex base coat, Ivy Green, Fern Green and Hunter Green*)
- Brushes—nos. 8, 16 golden natural flats, no. 1 script liner brush
- Design presses—commercially made or hand-cut from dense foam with craft knife
- Markers—permanent paint markers (optional)
- Palette and palette knife
- Acrylic glazing medium
- Toothbrush (optional)

Keys to Success

❋ Apply a light application of color to the design press. Excessive amounts of paint on the surface will cause the pattern to look smeared and blotchy when you press the surface.

❋ The background must be a flat base paint. Satin, semigloss and gloss surfaces will cause paint to bead up and slide around, causing the pattern to be out of focus.

❋ You can load part of the press with paint to achieve a partial impression (for example, half or one-fourth of a leaf).

❋ Don't be afraid to blend several shades or different colors on the press for tonal variations in the design.

❋ Several stamps with the press design will create an abundance of values: Lighter elements will appear to fade and recede, and darker impressions will come forward and be in brighter focus.

DESIGN PRESSES

STEP 1. Thin all colors to a flowing consistency with acrylic glazing medium. Depending on the size of the design press, load either a no. 8 or 16 flat brush with color. Stroke the flat area of the design press. You can load with one color or multivalues of one color or multihues. Blend lightly with the flat brush to intermingle color mixtures on the design press's pad. Place pad with paint side down, and lightly press your fingers around the surface to make impression. Try not to move pad while applying pressure; this will cause a blurred look.

STEP 2. Make several impressions with one application of color to create different values within the overall design. Now, load and press on some different-sized shapes for variety. To create a flowing design, follow some classic design forms, such *C* or *S* designs. You can also form linear designs for borders. Try to relate the shape of your design to the shape of the furniture section.

DESIGN PRESSES

STEP 3. To create a partial impression, only paint one-fourth to one-half of the design press with paint. This is especially effective when trying to create the feel that a leaf or flower element is turning away from the viewer. To create a stronger depth to the design, you can recoat or re-press the same pad design after the first is dried.

STEP 4. Connect design elements with the use of liner work. This can be completed with a permanent paint marker or by loading the script liner brush with thin, inklike-consistency paint. For leaf or floral motifs, add branches, stems or tendrils. Light flyspecking can also relax the design overall. To flyspeck, load a toothbrush with thin consistency paint, point the bristles toward the surface, and run your thumb over the toothbrush's bristles to let the paint flecks fall to the surface.

CHAPTER 7
DECORATIVE TECHNIQUES

New Decoupage
Trompe l'oeil
Tonal and Gradation
Masking and Ruling

The decoration of furniture can be accomplished through many different methods. To decorate means simply to dress up the surface or interior, changing it from a plain look to one that is more attractive. The end goal is to add elements to enhance the overall appearance and cause the viewer's eyes to be attracted to the furniture piece. The four techniques taught in this chapter provide you with a diversity of approaches to furniture decoration.

Like chapter six, two of the four techniques are abstract and graphic in the finished result (tonal and gradation, masking and ruling), while the other two are subject-matter oriented (new decoupage, trompe l'oeil). No matter which of these four you choose to refinish your furniture, an attractive decorative treatment will be achieved.

NEW DECOUPAGE

Today, an old craft form of decoupage is enjoying a revival. It is an ideal way to decorate a surface with colorful imagery of printed materials. You can use prints that have specifically been produced for use in decoupage or find printed materials, such as postcards, posters or fine art prints, to cut out and design with. Decoupage prints can be used in several ways—in an overlapping montage layout, centralized, or repeated in a border fashion.

Decoupage can be designed on furniture and accessories to be placed in virtually any room of the home. Depending on what type of printed material you are dealing with, you can design anything from elegance to country.

PREPARATION

Prime and seal the surface you wish to decoupage. Base coat the surface

Optional decoupage subject matter: right, ivy painted prints are cut out and placed in arc; center, celestial painted prints are cut out and scattered; left, bow and tassel painted prints are placed in linear form.

in a semigloss base paint of the color of your choice. Even if you plan on creating a montage effect (entire area covered with prints), you'll need to base coat the surface to provide a semislick surface to work on. You also may not end up covering small sections with prints so the base color will camouflage these open holes. Choose a base color that will relate to the most prominent color in your prints.

MATERIALS NEEDED:

- Paints—desired base color in acrylic or latex semigloss (*Sample project features Forest Green base coat*)
- Brushes—sponge brush, varnish brush
- Decoupage prints—commercially produced (for example, *Today's Decoupage Print no. 16016 Sunflowers by Back Street*) or hand-cut prints
- Decoupage glue
- Decoupage scissors—curved and straight blades
- Craft knife
- Ruler
- Chalk
- Water base polyurethane varnish
- Kitchen sponge
- Brayer

Keys to Success

✿ Always cut out more objects than you feel you will need. This will provide you with more elements to work with when designing and laying out your project.

✿ Turn the paper print when cutting the print versus turning the scissors. This will provide the cut paper edge with a sharper and cleaner look.

✿ Experiment with the layout of the prints before gluing them down. Take a piece of chalk and loosely draw an outline once the prints are in a pleasing position.

✿ Straight cuts can be easily achieved with a metal ruler and a craft knife. Curved cutting should be executed with a pair of curved scissors.

STEP 1. Cut out prints that are a part of a larger sheet into smaller sections that will be easier to handle when cutting the individual pieces (usually a piece no larger than 8″ × 10″). Using curved scissors for curved sections and straight blade scissors for linear areas, cut out desired shapes. Use a craft knife and ruler for exacting straight edges (for example, points of a star). Remember, when using the scissors, turn the paper into the cutting edge of the scissors; don't turn the scissors.

STEP 2. Determine positions for the cutout prints. You can mark these placements with chalk, if necessary. Brush glue onto the back of the print using the sponge brush. Turn print over, place on surface, and immediately smooth out the print with a damp kitchen sponge. A rubber brayer is also helpful in smoothing out the print and squeezing excess glue from under the print. Be sure all the edges are securely in place.

STEP 3. To create a montage effect, you'll continue to layer the surface with prints. Be sure to leave the central area of your working surface open for a final, larger overlapping print. This will create a nice focal point and center of interest. When you are finished gluing prints, complete one last check to see if all the print edges are glued in place. If any have popped up, place a small amount of glue on a no. 4 round brush and slide it under the print. Let prints dry overnight.

STEP 4. Seal and finish the prints with a series of coats of water base polyurethane varnish. You can place as many coats of varnish as you desire on the surface. In today's style of decoupage, it is not considered necessary to sink the print with twenty-five to thirty coats of finish. Three coats of varnish are plenty to protect prints and level out some of the prints' dimension.

TROMPE L'OEIL

The term *trompe l'oeil* is French and means "to fool the eye." In painted decoration, trompe l'oeil will fool the viewer into believing that something that is made from paint is true to life. In this technique presented here, you can combine reality with paint in an effective way that does not require great rendering skills.

The technique taught here is designed for a card table, but the subject matter could easily be changed to feminine, floral postcards for a totally different look. This quick and easy style of trompe l'oeil can be designed for many rooms of the home, including children's bedrooms, playrooms and feminine dressing rooms. Your reference material will direct the style of the project.

PREPARATION

Prime and seal the furniture surface. To create the light wood-grain effect with playing cards, base coat the surface with a cream-colored flat acrylic or latex paint. Brush on several coats with a base coat bristle brush. Sand lightly between coats until a smooth coverage is achieved. Remove the sanding dust with a tack rag.

Optional trompe l'oeil techniques: right, the surface was antiqued first with Burnt Umber and cards placed over; center, cards were placed then antiquing occurred; left, cards were antiqued first then placed on the surface.

MATERIALS NEEDED:

- Paints—desired base color in acrylic or latex flat; artist's acrylic color (*Sample project features Ecru base coat, Indian Brown glaze, Burnt Umber, Mars Black*)
- Brushes—glaze brush, flogger brush, nos. 8, 14 and 16 golden natural flats, no. 1 script liner brush, sponge brush
- Acrylic glazing medium
- Decoupage scissors—curved and straight blades
- Decoupage glue
- Kitchen sponge
- Brayer
- Color copies of subject matter
- Chalk (optional)
- Palette
- Palette knife

Keys to Success

- ✼ To complete this simple style of trompe l'oeil, choose flat objects that would normally rest on a furniture surface—postcards, playing cards, letters, children's drawings and other similar memorabilia.
- ✼ Don't be afraid to exaggerate shadows and highlights on the subjects. This will cause the viewers to take notice and get fooled when they try to pick up the painted attachments.
- ✼ Color copiers can change color dramatically. Be careful that color does not look unnatural.

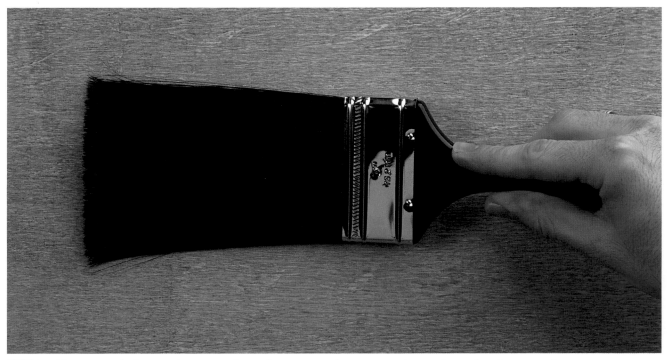

STEP 1. To create a light wood grain on the surface, mix earth tones together with acrylic glazing medium to a transparent color mixture. Brush on surface with a glaze brush. While the glaze is still wet, hit the surface with the flogger brush in a tapping and hopping motion. A fine pattern of dashlike wood grain marks will appear on the surface.

STEP 2. Use color copies of the objects you wish to feature on the surface; this will create less dimension, especially on overlapping elements. Cut out images with straight or curved blade scissors. Be sure to complete crisp, clean cuts so the objects appear realistic in shape.

STEP 3. Lay cutouts on the surface for positioning, and mark with chalk if a complex layout is designed. Place glue on the back of the copies with a sponge brush. Adhere print to the surface by smoothing it out with a moist kitchen sponge and brayer. Let dry overnight.

STEP 4. Create shadows around objects by thinning brown and black tones with water. Dip a flat brush in water, and blot on a paper towel. Side load one half of the flat brush in the thin consistency paint, and stroke on the palette to soften the blend on the brush. The loaded brush should have strong color on one side and fade away into the clean water side. A soft color gradation should be achieved where no visible color line exists. Stroke dark color against the bottom of the object's edge. On overlapping objects, place a shadow between them in a gray tone.

TONAL AND GRADATION

To complete this technique, you will create successive tones that slowly blend from one value into another. An illusionistic quality of dimension can be created when mingling the color tones on the surface. You will want to develop a softness to the paint by blending the values of one color or several colors carefully.

A light, airy feel is developed through this technique, so relaxed, casual rooms, such as bedrooms, dens and porches, are best suited for this look. This technique is also easily applied to wall surfaces.

PREPARATION

Prime the surface to be painted. Choose a midvalue color to base coat the furniture surface. Apply a semigloss acrylic or latex base coat to the surface. Apply several coats until an opaque coverage is achieved. Sand lightly between coats, and remove sanding dust with a tack rag. Mark off with pencil and ruler the areas to receive gradation. Mask surrounding areas with repositionable tape.

Optional color ways to use tone and gradation: right, three shades of white plus Hooker's Green plus Raw Umber are blended; center, three shades of white plus Yellow Ochre are blended; left, three shades of Phthalo Green plus white are blended.

MATERIALS NEEDED:
- Paints—desired base color in acrylic or latex semi-gloss; artist's acrylic colors (*Sample project features Sky Blue base coat, three values of Dark Williamsburg glaze, white*)
- Brushes—base coat bristle brush, glaze brush, blending softener brush
- Repositionable tape
- Pencil
- Ruler

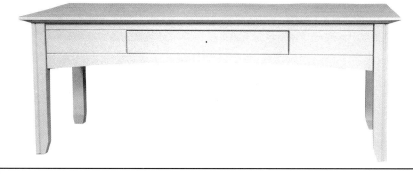

Keys to Success

❀ Be sure to premix a range of color values before applying color on the surface. You should mix at least a light, medium and dark value of every color you intend to use. If your values jump from very dark to very light, you'll end up with a splotchy look.

❀ Don't try to achieve an even blend on the first application; you'll need to recoat the surface to develop proper color placement, opacity, and a smooth blending of color.

❀ When completing the final blend, use a light touch on the blending softener brush. You should literally dust the surface; when you see paint move, don't apply any more pressure.

TONAL AND GRADATION

STEP 1. Create at least three values of the colors you choose. Begin with a dark value and add white to create lighter shades. Add acrylic glazing medium to all three values to create a thick, creamy consistency. Load the glaze brush with one color at a time, and stroke on color in a crisscross motion. You can place color values on the surface going from dark values on the outside edges of the surface toward lighter values in the center, or you can also place the colors in more of a random "sky" pattern.

STEP 2. Using the base coat bristle brush, loosely break up the distinct color division lines. You are not going after a final finish at this point. These first two steps are a blocking in of your color values. This will help you establish the overall look of the tonal and gradation. Let dry and evaluate the placement of tones.

STEP 3. Recoat the surface with the paint values. Place them in approximately the same areas as the first placement of colors. The second level of color will be easier for you to develop quickly because the first layer is the foundation. The second layer of color values will now create an opacity to the surface.

STEP 4. While the second layer of colors is still wet, use the blending softener brush to soften one color value into another. Use a light dusting action to mingle colors, but do not create mud. You want to achieve a subtle look between values and not leave a lot of heavy, visible brush marks on the surface. Let dry. Remove tape and clean up any overstrokes with base paint.

MASKING AND RULING

There is no greater way to design a clean, bold graphic look to a piece of furniture than through the use of the technique of masking and ruling. You can take an old, outdated piece of furniture and create a face-lift instantly. The masking part of the technique creates the broader areas of color shapes, while the ruling work defines the sections and trims out the work.

The masking and ruling work tends to develop a strong, masculine look, so it would be ideal when placed on furniture for a home of-

Optional color ways to use masking and ruling: right, Midnight Blue base with Light Gray panel and Light Green ruling; center, Red Oxide base with Coral panel and Light Brown ruling; left, Sand base with White panel and Burnt Sienna ruling.

fice, den, bedroom or library. A modern kitchen decor is also an excellent place to use the masking and ruling techniques—a great way to modernize old built-in cabinets.

PREPARATION

Prime and seal the furniture surface. Base coat the areas to receive masking and ruling with a flat acrylic or latex base paint. Apply several coats until an opaque coverage is achieved. Be sure to sand between coats to achieve a letter-perfect smooth finish.

Keys to Success

❋ Take your time in marking off the areas and shapes you wish to mask. Once painted, inconsistent shapes will be magnified.

❋ Be sure to burnish the tape edge properly. Paint can easily seep under improperly positioned tape.

❋ Always paint along the side of the tape; never stroke paint into the tape's edge. The latter will cause paint seepage.

❋ Test ruling pen on a scrap surface before drawing line work on the surface. If paint stops and starts, the paint is too thick. If paint blobs out, the consistency is too thin.

MATERIALS NEEDED:

- Paints—desired base color in acrylic or latex flat; artist's acrylic colors (*Sample project features Terra Cotta base coat, Forest Green trim, Black, Copper*)
- Brushes—base coat bristle brush, no. 4 golden natural round brush
- Repositionable tape
- Burnishing tool
- Ruler with raised edge
- Pencil
- Craft knife
- Palette
- Palette knife

MASKING AND RULING

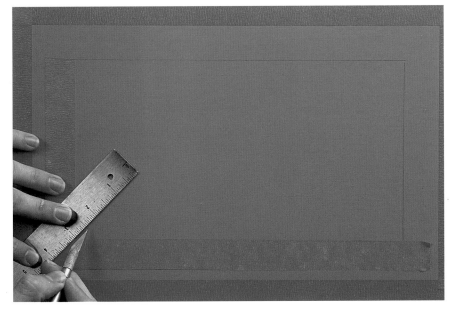

STEP 1. Mark off areas to be masked with pencil and ruler. Make light markings as guidelines for tape placement. Lay down repositionable tape to form masked-out shapes. For a clean, sharp outside corner, miter where two pieces of tape come together by lightly scoring the tape with a craft knife and ruler at a 45° angle. Remove excess tape from corner. With a burnishing tool, rub down the tape edges along which paint will be stroked.

STEP 2. Stroke paint along taped edge. When you come to a corner, turn the brush to follow the direction of the tape edge. Remember, stroke into the tape edge as little as possible to prevent paint seepage. Let first coat dry thoroughly, and recoat to achieve an opaque coverage. Let dry. Remove tape by pulling away from the painted edge. If paint starts to pull up, score tape or paint edge with craft knife.

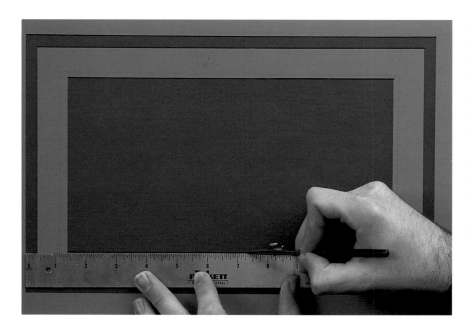

STEP 3. Thin the ruling line work color with water. The paint consistency should be slightly thicker than ink. Load the no. 4 round brush with color, and stroke along the ruling pen's open slotted area to fill with paint. Clean excess paint off sides of pen with towel. Hold pen at a 45° angle, and stroke on the palette surface. The paint should easily flow, forming a consistent line. Position raised ruler along painted area, and draw a colored line. Complete all horizontal lines. Let dry.

STEP 4. After all horizontal lines are dry, complete vertical lines. Hold pen at 45° angle, and stroke on surface. If you have problems meeting exactly at your corner intersections, it is advisable to go past the intersection. It is easy to touch up the overrun with some of the base paint and a script liner brush.

CHAPTER 8
FINISHING TECHNIQUES

Spray Finish
Brush Finish
Paste Wax Finish

Finishing techniques should not be overlooked for they are an important conclusion to the many hours of work you've put into the decorative techniques on your furniture piece. A good finish protects the work that went onto the surface, brings colors that dried dull and dark back to life, and creates a great deal of visual depth to the work. There is nothing like the feel of a superb finish on a piece of furniture. Admirers will be drawn to the surface, will want to touch and rub the surface, and will marvel at the quality of professionalism you've brought to your decorative work.

You can finish a surface with many different approaches. This chapter will instruct you on three of the most common and successful finishes that relate well to the furniture surface. They are as follows: a spray finish, a brush finish, and a paste wax finish. You can build these three types of finishes to multilevels if you desire a great deal of depth to the underlying work, or you can simply apply the necessary quantity of coats to seal and protect the work.

Finishing techniques don't require a lot of fancy tools. You'll need finishes: spray-on varnish, brush-on varnish, paste wax; smoothing agents: fine grades of sandpaper, steel wool, paper bags; and tools: varnish brushes, soap, water, cheesecloth, tack cloth, rags.

SPRAY FINISH

A finish that is applied by spraying can be a quick and easy technique. You must realize that a spray finish will protect the surface but often is not as tough as a finish applied by brush. You can achieve a thicker, more protective coating by brushing than by spraying. That is not to say that a spray finish does not have its merits; it can often be the best choice in your finishing techniques. The best use of a spray finish is on surfaces with many recessed areas that are hard to reach and surfaces that are cylindrical in shape. These can be difficult to brush a finish on and not achieve runs, so a spray-on finish is ideal in these cases.

Keys to Success

❋ A spray finish must be built up slowly. If you rush the application of the spray varnish, several problems will result: spray runs, a reaction of cracking and crazing or paint liftoff.

❋ Always test a product you've never used before on a scrap surface that has the same type of products and paints as used on your finished surface. All paints and products are not compatible and can cause serious problems and reactions.

❋ Apply spray finishes in well-ventilated areas. Use paint masks if you are sensitive to these types of smells.

❋ Build up spray finish very slowly with light mistings. Follow the drying schedule between coats that's recommended on the label's instructions.

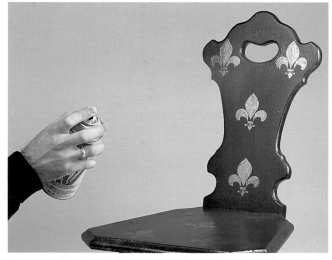

STEP 1. Apply a light misting of spray finish to the surface. Hold the can 10" to 12" away from the surface. Start at the top of the surface, stroking from the left side of the surface to the right and back again. Overlap each sweep slightly. Remember to dust the surface lightly. Don't gum the surface with finish. Let dry. Repeat several applications until you can see a leveling of the sheen on the surface. It is best to develop eight to ten light mistings than two to three heavy coats. Let cure thoroughly before proceeding.

STEP 2. To remove any slight texture that may have occurred when you were spraying on the finish, you'll need to buff the surface. Cut a small piece of a brown grocery sack to lightly buff and "sand" the surface. This brown sack is less coarse than some of the finer sandpaper and will not cut through the spray finish. Using a swirling motion, you'll lightly buff the surface. Remove any paper particles with a tack rag. Complete the finish with two light coatings of the spray finish.

BRUSH FINISH

A finish developed through the application of a series of brush-applied coats can achieve a great deal of depth in the furniture surface. Multiple coats may take a longer time to develop due to the extensive drying time required between coats, but often the finished result far outweighs the time involved. If you wish to build a glasslike finish on the surface, then a brush finish is for you. Be sure to use a varnish finish that is water stain and alcohol resistant so you can use it on "active" furniture surfaces.

Keys to Success

❋ A water base varnish that is polyurethane based will provide you with the greatest amount of durability. These varnishes often have superior leveling properties that will smooth out as they dry.

❋ This finish should be brushed on in a fluid coating. Applied too dryly, a varnish can show visible brush marks; applied too heavily, runs and sagging will occur.

❋ A soft, natural hair varnish brush will yield the best result. A foam brush can be used, but since the foam brush soaks up so much varnish, it can be difficult to control.

❋ Never shake a varnish container; gently stir the contents. Excessive movement inside the container can cause air bubbles to form that can be transferred to the furniture surface.

❋ When completing wet sanding techniques, please be aware that you can sand and cut through the three layers of varnish very quickly. Use a light touch and caution.

❋ For a glasslike finish, you can apply a series of varnish coats and wet sand between each series. For example: Apply three coats; wet sand; apply three more coats; wet sand; apply two more coats, wet sand; finish with one final coat for a total of nine coats of finish.

STEP 1. Using a natural hair varnish brush, float on a smooth, level coating of water base polyurethane varnish. Start from one side of the surface and stroke across, overlapping each stroke slightly. Don't make short strokes; try to stroke fluidly across the surface from one side to another. On a larger piece, work one section at a time (for example, drawer front, side panel). Allow first coat to dry and cure following manufacturer's instructions. Recoat a second and third time.

STEP 2. To level out and smooth the finish, wet sand the surface. Use 600-grit wet/dry fine black sandpaper. Dip sandpaper in water, and then stroke across a bar of soap. Using a circular motion, lightly sand the surface. The water and soap move the sanding particles away. You can cut down to the decorative finishes very quickly—use caution. Complete only one pass across the surface. Wipe away sanding particles, soap and water with a clean paper towel. The surface will now appear hazy and scratched. This will go away when you recoat with a final coat of brush-on varnish.

PASTE WAX FINISH

There is no better way to achieve a hand-rubbed and handcrafted finish than through the use of paste wax. Stained finishes that show off the beauty of a wood grain are ideal to top off with a paste wax coat. A certain patina develops as you layer a paste wax over the surface. One aspect to keep in mind is this finish has a minimum level of protection to the decorative work below. You can use the paste wax technique over a spray finish or brush finish as an extra step for heavy-duty protection to the surface below. However, if you wish to keep the tactile qualities of the decorative paint treatment close to the top surface and are not concerned with maximum protection, a paste wax finish is for your piece of furniture.

STEP 1. Apply an even coating of paste wax to the furniture surface with a piece of cheesecloth. Coat surface with a circular motion. When working on a large surface, you may want to complete both steps before proceeding to a new section. On a smaller piece, you can coat entire surface and then buff entire surface. If you wish to age the surface, rub on a coating of tinted paste wax. Let wax dry, forming a white, hazy look.

Keys to Success

❋ Don't go overboard when applying the paste wax coating on the surface. A thick coating is more difficult to buff out and bring to a level finish. Excessive wax also makes the surface feel greasy.

❋ Let the wax set up the required amount of time before buffing. This will ensure the best-looking results.

❋ You can tint the paste wax with color to age the underlying work. Mix a small amount of color into the wax with a palette knife, and proceed as normal.

❋ You should recoat the surface with a fresh coating of paste wax in about a year. The wax can soak into some porous wood surfaces over time.

STEP 2. After the hazy look has appeared, begin buffing. Using a clean, soft, cotton rag and a lot of "elbow grease," buff the surface in a circular motion. The more buff action and friction that occurs, the greater the sheen will appear. Complete this step on all sections that are coated with wax. Step back and look for inconsistent spots of dull or glossy areas. Bring dull areas up by buffing with the cloth. Tone down glossy areas by lightly hitting the surface with ultrafine steel wool.

CHAPTER 9
PATTERN IDEAS

The following patterns are provided for you to use as guidelines for your furniture decoration. These designs are used in the foil gilding, fleur de lis pattern; stenciling, ABCs—apple, boat and cat; design presses, ivy patterns. The patterns could be used in the creation of stencils, cut sponge designs or gilding, or they could be hand painted. If you wish to use one of these designs, simply trace the design from the book with tracing paper and a fine line black marker. To gild or paint the design, center the traced design onto your surface and tape in place. Slip a sheet of gray graphite or white transfer paper underneath, and trace lightly over the lines of the design to transfer it to your surface. Trace and transfer the basic outlines only. Now you're ready to hand paint or gild. To create stencils or design presses, see respective chapters.

CHAPTER 10 SHOWCASE

The following examples of finished painted effects for furniture and accessories will provide you with a wealth of reference materials. Remember, experimentation is the key to coming up with unique solutions for the furniture project at hand. Use these examples as inspiration. You don't need to copy them exactly; the shape and style and desired coloration of your piece may be totally different from what is shown here. Work up some variations on sample boards before beginning your furniture decoration project. Good luck.

A Distressed Kitchen

A kitchen renovation project features the distressing technique applied to both old and new kitchen cabinets. First, new, unfinished cabinets were stained to match existing cabinets, then all cabinets were painted in a taupe color. Heavy distressing was completed with sandpaper, hammer, screwdriver, nails and screws. Distressing dust was removed with tack rags. To soften the look, a transparent cream glaze was brushed over the cabinets, then the excess glaze was wiped off with rags.

Marquetry Floors

A bold, graphic pattern of diamonds, lines, borders and a central medallion enhance this sitting room's floor. The existing stained floors were sanded to remove all stain and varnish coating. The design was then marked on the raw wood with fine pencil lines. Individual sections were taped off, one area at a time. Then, gel stains of Burnt Umber, Burnt Sienna, Yellow Ochre and Black were rubbed into the raw wood. Fine lines were completed with a permanent marker to outline and define all sections. A series of varnish coats were applied to seal and protect.

Floral Coffee Table

Often a piece of furniture may only need the addition of a decorative design. Here, this coffee table's existing finish was in excellent shape. A fabric floral design was the inspiration for the decorative painting completed on the tabletop. To create this effect, trace sections of floral designs from fabric or wallpaper with pencil and tracing paper. Mix up a palette of colors to match reference material. Paint the subject matter similar to the fabric but don't copy it.

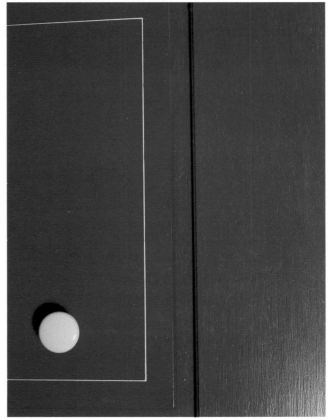

Bright Red Kitchen

Colorful stenciling of fruits and leaves was executed over glazed walls of gray and white. Cabinets, doors and molding were painted in a flogged finish of a rich red glaze over a hot pink base coat. White ruling pen line work was applied to create a sharp, crisp trim.

A Nasturtium Kitchen

A fabric pattern of nasturtiums was the starting point for the decorative painting on the table and floorcloths. A rich palette of greens, terra cottas, reds and salmons transform a previously dark kitchen. Cabinets were glazed in two shades of green. Table and chairs were antiqued with a midvalue green over white and enhanced with decoratively painted nasturtiums. Matching floorcloths were completed with masking, ruling and glazing techniques.

Wet Bar Vineyard

This small wet bar room features
painted cabinets, walls and accessories.
A mural features stone arches entwined
with grapes, vines and leaves. Textured
walls were glazed with a series of earth
tone glazes. Cabinets, glazed in two
shades of green, gilded with a grape
motif. The column was antiqued in
Burnt Umber, Raw Umber and Burnt
Sienna over a Cream base coat.

Gilded Serving Tray

This metal serving tray was first base coated in black. The grape design was transferred, and then gold finish was applied to the surrounding areas. Adhesive was painted where gold was to be applied. Gold foil was burnished on the adhesive areas. Fine ruling pen lines of black were marked to trim grape band areas. The entire tray was then antiqued in a Burnt Umber glaze. A high-gloss finish was applied to round out the elegant look.

Gilded Accessories

The quick and easy method of foil gilding trims out a few accessories. Adhesive and gold were applied to the grame, lamp base and mask. Light antiquing was completed on the frame and mask in earth tone glaze, while heavy antiquing was completed on the lamp base to almost disguise the gold finish. A spray finish in a high gloss was easily applied to these dimensional pieces.

Fruit-Inspired Kitchen

This kitchen features several techniques applied to a variety of surfaces—furniture, cabinets, floor and accessories. A set of kitchen table and chairs features a blue distressed finish with decoratively painted fruit. The floorcloth was completed with masking and ruling techniques, and then the complementing fruit design was applied. Kitchen cabinets were painted in a gray blue and glazed with an off-white.

Torn Paper Walls

The walls of this room feature the torn paper technique. Sheets of paper were coated in two different shades of burgundy and torn into individual pieces. The paper was then crumpled into a ball and straightened back out. A black transparent glaze was applied to stain the torn edges and catch in all the wrinkles. The paper was then installed on walls in an overlapping pattern with wallpaper paste. To seal and protect walls, a series of varnish coats were applied to create an attractive sheen.

Marble Tabletop

This colonial style ratchet table features two painted techniques—antiquing on the base and marbleizing on the top. The base of the table was painted in a burgundy base coat. It was then antiqued with a light pink with a little flyspecking. The tabletop was marbleized in light tones of cream, white and pink in a breccia (chunk) type marble pattern. The table was protected with nine varnish coats for an opulent finish.

CREDITS AND ACKNOWLEDGMENTS

The publisher and author would like to give credit and thanks to the individuals involved in creating the work featured within.

All color photography featured in chapters one through eight copyright © by Michael La Riche, La Riche Studios, 5225 Wilshire Blvd., Mezzanine, Los Angeles CA 90036; (213) 933-7885.

Artwork and step-by-step illustrations in chapters one through eight by Phillip C. Myer.

Pages 114-115: home of Mike Ottwhiler; interior decoration by Jackie Naylor; paint finishes by Andy Jones and Phillip C. Myer; photography by Andy Jones.

Pages 116-117: home of Mr. and Mrs. Wood; interior decoration by Carter Arnest; paint finishes by Andy Jones and Phillip C. Myer; photography by Andy Jones.

Page 118: painted table by Phillip C. Myer; photography by Andy Jones.

Page 119: offices of PCM Studios; paint finishes by Andy Jones and Phillip C. Myer; photography by Andy Jones.

Pages 120-121: home of Mr. and Mrs. Hinkle; interior decoration by PCM Studios; paint finishes by Andy Jones and Phillip C. Myer; photography by Andy Jones.

Page 122: wet bar at the Atlanta Symphony Decorator Show House; interior decoration by PCM Studios; paint finishes by Andy Jones and Phillip C. Myer; photography by David Shillings.

Page 123: painted tray by Phillip C. Myer; photography by David Shillings.

Page 123: gilding by Andy Jones; photography by David Shillings.

Pages 124-125: home of Mr. and Mrs. Ouzts; interior decoration by Neecy's Design; paint finishes by Andy Jones, Denise Ouzts and Phillip C. Myer; photography by David McCord.

Page 126: offices of PCM Studios; paint finishes by Phillip C. Myer; photography by Andy Jones.

Page 127: painted table by Phillip C. Myer; photography by Andy Jones.

SUGGESTED READING

Bennell, Jennifer. *Master Strokes.* Rockport, ME: Rockport Publishers, 1991.

Fales, Jr., Dean, A. *American Painted Furniture 1660-1880.* New York: Bonanza Books, 1986.

Fisher, Rosie. *Painting Furniture.* Boston: Little, Brown and Company, 1988.

Gray, Linda, and Jocasta Innes. *The Complete Book of Decorating Techniques.* Boston: Little, Brown and Company, 1986.

Hauser, Priscilla. *The Priscilla Hauser Book of Tole & Decorative Painting.* New York: Van Nostrand Reinhold Company, 1977.

———. *Folk Art Painting for Home Decoration.* New York: Prentice Hall, 1986.

Innes, Jocasta. *Decorating With Paint.* New York: Harmony Books, 1986.

———. *Painting Furniture.* New York: Pantheon Books, 1991.

Le Grice, Lyn. *The Stenciled House.* New York: Simon and Schuster, 1988.

Marx, Allen, Ina Marx, and Robert Marx. *Professional Painted Finishes.* New York: Watson-Guptill Publications, 1991.

Myer, Phillip C. *Creative Paint Finishes for the Home.* Cincinnati: North Light Books, 1992.

O'Neil, Isabel. *The Art of the Painted Finish for Furniture & Decoration.* New York: William Morrow & Company, 1971.

Ridley, Jessica. *Finishing Touches.* New York: Charles Scribner's Sons, 1988.

Sloan, Annie and Kate Gwynn. *Classic Paints & Faux Finishes.* New York: Reader Digest, 1993.

———. *The Completed Book of Decorative Paint Techniques.* New York: Portland House, 1989.

GLOSSARY

ABSTRACT—unrelated to reality in terms of painted finishes. The painted effect is not an imitation of natural objects.

ACRYLIC POLYMER—a thermoplastic resin, with a synthetic substance or mixture, used as a binder with powdered pigments in the creation of artist's acrylic colors.

ANTIQUING—the application of a very thin, transparent coating placed over a surface to provide the illusion of age and patina.

ARTIST'S ACRYLIC COLORS—paint that is a mixture of powdered pigments ground in thermoplastic, synthetic emulsions. They can be thinned and cleaned up with water.

BASE COAT—the initial application of paint to a surface.

BINDER—the agent that acts as a cohesive to join particles together. Binders hold powdered pigments together in artist's colors.

BODY—the weight or form of an object; as it relates to paint, the consistency.

BURNISH—to polish or to rub a surface with a hard tool, especially to adhere and smooth areas.

CHISEL—the sharp edge that forms on the end of a well-crafted flat brush.

CLEAR COAT—the application of a transparent sealing agent over a surface, most commonly placed over raw, untreated wood to seal the grain but not cover up the wood grain pattern.

COLOR VALUES—the degrees of lightness, darkness, saturation and brightness of a hue.

CORBELS—decorative accents made of plaster, pottery, wood or stone. They project out from the face of a wall or a furniture surface.

CRACKLED—when a surface shows random separations in its paint or varnish finish, making it appear older than it really is; can result from product incompatibility, temperature or weather.

CRAZING—the paint reaction (chemical incompatibility) caused on purpose or by accident that produces a fine pattern of cracks in the paint or varnish surface; can also be caused by temperature or exposure to weather.

CRISSCROSS—a paint stroke direction that forms crossed lines, overlapping randomly, making *X* shapes.

CURTAINING—the sagging or dripping of a layer of paint or varnish placed over a previous coat that is not cured and dried. The top layer weights down the first layer that is not dried and pulls both layers down like a sagging curtain.

DARK VALUE—the deeper color tones on the gray scale that can be created from any color by the addition of black or that color's complement on the color wheel.

DECORATIVE PAINTING—an ornamental art form used to decorate functional as well as nonfunctional surfaces. It is a teachable art form broken down into step-by-step methods.

DECOUPAGE—the French art form of cutting and pasting down images to form decorative treatments on a surface.

DISTRESSING—the action of battering a surface through the use of abrasive tools, such as sandpaper, hammer, nail, screw or chains. The goal is to imitate age and the wear and tear of a surface.

EARTH TONES—colors that are made with natural pigments (like yellow ochre, which is made from refined clay).

FAUX—the French word that translates as false or fake. As it relates to painted finishes, it defines a painted look that mimics a real surface, for example, faux marble, painted to look like marble; faux bois, painted to look like wood grain.

FERRULE—the metal section of a brush, which is crimped (pinched) together to hold the hairs of the brush. Note: The hairs of the brush go far up inside the metal section.

FLAT—paint sheen or finish that is dull and porous.

FLECKS—small particles of paint spattered on the surface.

FLYSPECKING—the painting technique that disperses small particles of paint over the surface with the use of a toothbrush and thin consistency paint.

FOIL GILDING—an inexpensive and quick technique using foil to achieve a similar look to traditional gilding technique with real or imitation metal leaf.

FREEHAND—to create without the use of patterns or guidelines.

GEL STAINING—to tint a raw wood surface with thick, creamy consistency stains that have a tremendous amount of body. Gel stains will not bleed; they hold a line.

GILDING—the application of gold, silver or copper leaf to a surface.

GLAZE—a transparent mixture of color plus a clear painting medium.

GLOSS—the highest level of a finish's sheen or shine qualities.

GOLD LEAF—real or imitation gold that has been hammered into extremely delicate sheets of five-millionths of an inch in thickness.

GRAY SCALE—a standardized chart of values from white to black (from lightest to darkest) in percentage increments.

GRID—a framed structure of equally spaced parallels and crossbars used to paint various tile or stripe patterns. A grid is also used to enlarge or reduce the size of designs by scaling them up or down proportionately.

HAZE—a transparent but cloudy or smoky coating over a surface that obstructs the clarity of the color below.

HIGH CONTRAST—an extreme color value difference in close proximity. The highest level would be from white to gray to black in a short distance.

HUE—the quality of color; the intensity of color, as in a shade or tint.

INKLIKE CONSISTENCY—paint thinned with painting medium, painting glaze or solvent to the liquid state that matches drawing ink.

LATEX—paint made from powdered pigments ground with emulsion of rubber or plastic globules. It can be cleaned with water.

LIFTOFF—the intentional or accidental removal of base coat, paint finish or varnish.

LIGHT VALUE—the brighter color values on the gray scale. Any color can become a light value by the addition of white.

MARBLEIZING—the act of reproducing a marble pattern through the use of paint applied with a brush or feathers on a surface.

MASKING—to mark off an area and then protect that area by covering with tape or other item so it won't receive paint when a nearby area is being painted.

MEDIUM—the type of paint used, such as acrylics or oils; a liquid, such as water base varnish, acrylic retarder and water, used to thin acrylic paints.

MEDIUM VALUE—a color tone that is not too dark and not too light; a shade in the middle from dark value to light value.

MIDTONE—a center point of a color's value in relation to its lightest or darkest points within a given painted area.

MONTAGE—to overlap design elements on a surface until very little or none of the original surface shows; a technique employed in decoupage.

MOSAIC—a decorative design made from small pieces of colored tile or colored glass (tessera) that are set into mortar.

MULTITONE—the development of a variety of values of one color or many colors on a surface.

OPAQUE—paint coverage thick enough that light cannot pass through it.

OPEN TIME—the period in which the paints, painting mediums or varnishes will remain workable before they begin to set up and dry.

PAINT RUNS—usually undesirable drips of paint or varnish that move down a vertical surface.

PASTE WAX—a coating of specially designed wax for furniture that is rubbed on and adds a level of polish and sheen to a surface.

PATINA—the marks and signs of age that develop on a surface, creating character often thought of as patina; the corrosion that occurs as metals oxidize.

PATTERN—a guideline to follow when creating, as in woodworking, sewing or decorative painting.

PICKLING—the staining and sealing of a raw wood surface with clean, clear colors, such as white, blue or green.

PLASTER—a substance made of a mixture of lime, sand and water. It is molded and formed into various architectural or decorative shapes.

POROUS—a surface that has permeable openings that moisture easily penetrates.

POTTERY—a substance made from earth and clay. It is molded, formed or thrown to create dimensional pieces, both functional and non-functional.

PRIMER—an opaque, paintlike base coat application that seals the surface and readies it for decorative treatment; a stain blocking sealer that does not allow bottom coats to penetrate through.

RETARDER—an agent that suspends and slows down the quick drying time of some water base products, such as acrylics.

RULING—the trim work of fine lines through the application of thin consistency paint with a ruling pen.

SAGGING—the lifting and dropping of a coat of paint due to improper surface preparation.

SATIN—a finish or surface with a slight amount of sheen or shine.

SEMIGLOSS—a finish or surface with a sheen level greater than satin but less than gloss.

SETUP TIME—the period it takes for the paint, painting glaze or varnish to begin to dry and become tacky.

SIDE LOAD—to carry color on one side of the brush with painting medium or solvent on the other, creating a blended transition on the brush from opaque color to transparent color to no color.

SOLVENT—the agent that cleans and thins, such as paints, varnishes and painting mediums. A paint's solvent can be used as a painting medium. The solvent for acrylic is water; the solvent for oils is turpentine.

SPACKLING COMPOUND—also called plaster patch; a thick-bodied, plasterlike substance used to fill holes in furniture.

SPONGING—the painted finish techniques that use the application of paint loaded on a sponge to create a textural pattern on a surface.

STENCIL—a sheet of Mylar, acetate or heavy card stock with a design cut into it.

STENCILING—the decorative application of design work achieved by brushing paint through a cut design opening.

STRIE—the painted finish technique that creates irregular linear streaks in a wet paint glaze through the use of a flogger brush.

STRIPING—the addition of horizontal or vertical lines (or a combination of both) in any degree of line width.

STRIPPING—the removal of paint, varnish or other buildup on a surface through the use of commercially made chemical products and scraping tools.

SUBSTRATUM—the base or foundation of a surface; what the surface is made from. For most furniture, it would be the raw wood.

TACKY—a sticky quality that develops during the drying time of a paint product. Some techniques require waiting for a tacky paint, glue or varnish state before proceeding with the technique.

TELEGRAPHING—the action of an impression or pattern coming up from a foundation level exposing itself to the top layers that were placed over it to cover it up.

THICK, CREAMY CONSISTENCY—a paint mixed with a very small amount of painting medium, paint glaze or solvent and whipped to the texture of whipped butter. Paint should hold peaks when patted with palette knife.

THIN, CREAMY CONSISTENCY—a paint mixed with painting medium, paint glaze or solvent to the texture of whipping cream.

THIN, SOUPY CONSISTENCY—a paint mixed with painting medium, paint glaze or solvent to the texture of watered-down soup.

TONAL AND GRADATION—the creation of various color tones that intermingle and go down the value scale in an even transition.

TONE ON TONE—the layering of subtle color values very close in lightness or darkness on the gray scale.

TORN PAPER—the paint finish technique that employs the use of painted and torn paper installed in a layering fashion.

TRANSPARENT—a coating of paint or glaze so thin that light can easily pass through. When something is transparent, you can see through it clearly.

TROMPE L'OEIL—the French term for "fool the eye"; a painting style that renders objects in life-size proportions, fooling the viewer into believing he or she is seeing real objects.

VALUE—the ratio or percentage of color that relates to the gray scale; a color from lightest to darkest.

VARNISH—a clear coating of either a water-based polyurethane or oil-based product that protects what is underneath the coating.

VEINS—the interior structural pattern element found in leaf structures and marble surfaces.

VENEER—a thin wood panel applied to a surface with glue coating.

WASH—paint that is thinned with enough painting medium, paint glaze or solvent to make it fluid and transparent.

WET SANDING—the smoothing of a surface with a fine, wet/dry style sandpaper that is wet with water and soap. This application is completed in the finishing stage, removing any imperfections between coats of varnish.

WOOD GRAIN—the pattern of marks found in wood surfaces; a flowing organic pattern.

WOOD GRAINING—the painted finish that duplicates a wood type through the use of a wet paint glaze, brushes and tools.

WOOD PUTTY—the thick compound made of whiting, linseed oil and binders in a doughlike consistency that is used to fill imperfections on a wood surface before painting or finishing.

SOURCES

The following companies are the manufacturers, mail-order suppliers or facilities that offer instructional materials or seminars that may be of interest to you. Please write for further information. Many times a stamped, self-addressed return envelop will get you a response.

These are the resources for the specific materials used in the creation of the decorated furniture found in this book:

BRUSHES

SILVER BRUSH LIMITED
5 Oxford Court
Princeton Junction NJ 08550
(609) 275-8691 Phone
(609) 275-1197 Fax

FURNITURE— UNFINISHED

KHOURY, INC.
2201 East Industrial Drive
P.O. Box 729
Iron Mountain MI 49801
(800) 553-5446 Phone
(906) 774-8211 Fax

GLAZES, GLUES, DESIGN PRESSES AND VARNISHES

BACK STREET, INC.
3905 Steve Reynolds Boulevard
Norcross GA 30093
(404) 381-7373 Phone
(404) 381-6424 Fax

PATINA PRODUCTS

MODERN OPTIONS
2325 Third Street, Suite 339
San Francisco CA 94107
(415) 252-5580 Phone
(415) 252-5599 Fax

Torn Paper Walls

In this bathroom, the torn paper technique was executed. The sheets of paper were first painted a deep forest green. Then, three lighter shades of green were individually sponged over the paper with a natural sea sponge. The paper was torn into random pieces. The torn paper edges were stained with a lighter green glaze. The paper was installed on walls with wallpaper paste. A protective coating of varnish was brushed on walls to seal.

PAINTS—ARTIST'S ACRYLICS, GEL MEDIUM, RETARDER

MARTIN F. WEBER COMPANY
2727 Southampton Road
Philadelphia PA 19154
(215) 677-5600 Phone
(215) 677-3336 Fax

TAPES AND STRIPPER

3M CONSUMER PRODUCTS GROUP
P.O. Box 33053
St Paul MN 55133
(612) 733-1110

The following companies' products and services may interest you.

ARTCRAFT WOOD SHOP
Highway 69A, Box 75
Crestline KS 66728
(316) 389-2574
Unfinished wood furniture and accessories

ARITOCAST ORIGINALS
6200 Highlands Parkway, Suite 1
Smyrna GA 30082
(404) 333-9934
Cast moldings of plaster

ADELE BISHOP, INC.
P.O. Box 3349
Kinston NC 28501
(919) 527-4189
Stencil supplies

DEE-SIGNS, LTD
P.O. Box 960
Newnan GA 30264
(404) 304-1993
Stencil supplies

GAIL GRISI STENCILING, INC.
P.O. Box 1263
Haddonfield NJ 08033
(609) 354-1757
Stencil supplies

HOUSE PARTS
479 Whitehall Street SW
Atlanta GA 30303
(404) 577-5584
Plaster cast objects

The following are schools that specialize in the teaching of paint and faux finishes for the decoration of furniture and interiors:

AMERICAN ACADEMY OF DECORATIVE FINISHES
14255 North Seventy-ninth Street
Suite 10
Scottsdale AZ 85260

DAY STUDIO WORKSHOP, INC.
1504 Bryant Street
San Francisco CA 94103

FINISHING SCHOOL, INC.
120 Woodbine Avenue
Northport NY 11768

PCM STUDIOS
School of the Decorative Arts
731 Highland Avenue NE, Suite D
Atlanta GA 30312

INDEX

More Great Books for Creating Beautiful Crafts

Creative Finishes Series—Explore the world of creative finishing with leading decorative artist, Phil Myer! Each book features a variety of techniques, paint applications and surface treatments in 15 projects complete with detailed instructions, patterns and step-by-step photos.

Painting & Decorating Tables—#30910/ $23.99/112 pages/177 color illus./paperback

Painting & Decorating Boxes—#30911/ $23.99/112 pages/145 color, 32 b&w illus./ paperback

Painting & Decorating Cabinets & Chests—#31116/$23.99/112 pages/163 color illus./paperback

The Crafter's Guide to Pricing Your Work—Price and sell more than 75 kinds of crafts with this must-have reference. You'll learn how to set prices to maximize income while maintaining a fair profit margin. Includes tips on record-keeping, consignment, taxes, reducing costs and managing your cash flow. #70353/$16.99/160 pages/paperback

Painting & Decorating Birdhouses—Turn unfinished birdhouses into something special—from a quaint Victorian roost to a Southwest pueblo, from a rustic log cabin to a lighthouse! These colorful and easy decorative painting projects are for the birds with 22 clever projects to create indoor decorative birdhouses, as well as functional ones to grace your garden. #30882/$23.99/128 pages/194 color illus./paperback

The Art of Painting Animals on Rocks—Discover how a dash of paint can turn humble stones into charming "pet rocks." This hands-on easy-to-follow book offers a menagerie of fun—and potentially profitable—stone animal projects. Eleven examples, complete with material lists, photos of the finished piece and patterns will help you create a forest of fawns, rabbits, foxes and other adorable critters. #30606/ $21.99/144 pages/250 color illus./paperback

Painting More Animals on Rocks—Lin Wellford has introduced thousands of people to the unique magic of transforming ordinary rocks into imaginative words of art. The fun continues in this book as Lin shows you how to become your own "rock artist" by creating frogs, penguins, field mice, foals, bears, wolves and other colorful creatures. #31108/$21.99/128 pages/ 290 color illus./paperback

Making Greeting Cards With Rubber Stamps—Discover hundreds of quick, creative, stamp-happy ways to make extra-special cards—no experience, fancy equipment or expensive materials required! You'll find 30 easy-to-follow projects for holidays, birthdays, thank you's and more! #30821/$21.99/128 pages/231 color illus./paperback

Acrylic Decorative Painting Techniques—Discover stroke-by-stroke instruction that takes you through the basics and beyond! More than 50 fun and easy painting techniques are illustrated in simple demonstrations that offer at least two variations on each method. Plus, a thorough discussion on tools, materials, color, preparation and backgrounds. #30884/$24.99/ 128 pages/550 color illus.

The Decorative Stamping Sourcebook—Embellish walls, furniture, fabric and accessories—with stamped designs! You'll find 180 original, traceable motifs in a range of themes and illustrated instructions for making your own stamps to enhance any decorating style. #30898/ $24.99/128 pages/200 color illus.

Master Strokes—Master the techniques of decorative painting with this comprehensive guide! Learn to use decorative paint finishes on everything from small objects and furniture to walls and floors, including dozens of step-by-step demonstrations and numerous techniques. #30937/ $22.99/160 pages/400 color illus./paperback

Decorative Painting Sourcebook—Priscilla Hauser, Phillip Myer and Jackie Shaw lend their expertise to this one-of-a-kind guide straight from the pages of Decorative Artist's Workbook! You'll find step-by-step, illustrated instructions on every technique—from basic brushstrokes to faux finishes, painting glassware, wood, clothing and much more! #30883/$24.99/128 pages/ 200 color illus./paperback

Paper Craft—Dozens of step-by-step paper craft projects to make, including greeting cards, boxes and desk sets, jewelry and pleated paper blinds. If you have ever worked with or wanted to work with paper you'll enjoy these attractive, fun-to-make projects. #30530/$16.99/144 pages/200 color illus./ paperback

Everything You Ever Wanted to Know About Fabric Painting—Discover how to create beautiful fabrics! You'll learn how to set up workspace, choose materials, plus the ins and outs of tie-dye, screen printing, woodgraining, marbling, cyanotype and more! #30625/$21.99/128 pages/4-color throughout/paperback

Stencil Source Book 2—Add color and excitement to fabrics, furniture, walls and more with over 200 original motifs that can be used again and again! Idea-packed chapters will help you create dramatic color schemes and themes to enhance your home in hundreds of ways. #30730/$22.99/144 pages/300 illus.

1,200 Paint Effects for the Home Decorator—Here is a practical, visual color and mix directory of 1,200 fantastic paint finishes for your home. Take the guesswork out of finding the ideal color combination or paint effect for any kind of job. #30949/$29.99/192 pages/ 1,200+ color illus.

Trompe L'Oeil: Creating Decorative Illusions with Paint—Learn the art of "tricking the eye" by following these eight fully illustrated projects that create the illusion of three-dimensional space on a flat surface. Each project contains traceable motifs and start-to-finish instructions for creating realistic decorative effects for your walls—from architectural elements to scenery, still lifes to drapery. #31130/$27.99/144 pages/250 color illus.

The North Light Book of Creative Paint Finishing Techniques—This beautifully illustrated book features more than 45 professional finishing techniques for decorating walls, cabinets, mantels, window frames, moldings and more. Plenty of hands-on instruction makes this a good book for beginners as well as amateurs. #31109/$29.99/144 pages/500+ color illus.

Creative Paint Finishes for the Home—Phil Myer's companion volume to his bestselling Creative Paint Finishes for Furniture is a complete full-color, step-by-step guide to decorating floors, walls and furniture—including how to use the tools, master the techniques and develop your own ideas. #30426/$27.99/144 pages/212 color illus.

Making Money with Your Creative Paint Finishes—If you've mastered faux finishing, stenciling or mural painting, your skills are in high demand. Armed with the smart-business advice featured in this new guide, you can turn your talents into profit by starting your own successful decorative finishing enterprise. #31110/ $18.99/160 pages/paperback